WISCONSIN
Curiosities

Help Us Keep This Guide Up to Date

Every effort has been made by the authors and editors to make this guide as accurate and useful as possible. However, many things can change after a guide is published—establishments close, phone numbers change, facilities come under new management, and so forth.

We would love to hear from you concerning your experiences with this guide and how you feel it could be made better and kept up to date. While we may not be able to respond directly to your comments and suggestions, we'll take them to heart, and we'll also make certain to share them with the authors. Please send your comments and suggestions to the following address:

The Globe Pequot Press
Reader Response/Editorial Department
P.O. Box 480
Guilford, CT 06437

Or you may e-mail us at:
editorial@GlobePequot.com

Thanks for your input, and happy travels!

Curiosities Series

WISCONSIN
Curiosities

Quirky Characters, Roadside Oddities & Other Offbeat Stuff

Second Edition

Michael Feldman
and Diana Cook

The
Globe
Pequot
Press

GUILFORD, CONNECTICUT

The prices, rates, and hours listed in this book were confirmed at press time. We recommend, however, that you call establishments to obtain current information before traveling.

Cover design by Nancy Freeborn
Cover photos: *front cover:* (bottom right) Jerry Minnich; (bottom left) John Wall, SMSU Photographic Services; (middle) courtesy National Freshwater Fishing Hall of Fame; (top) Rick Serocki

Page design by Bill Brown
Page layout by Deborah Nicolais

Photo credits: pp. viii, 10, 66, 71, 225: © Andy Kraushaar; pp. 2, 62, 82, 85, 92, 99, 107, 113, 124, 134, 147, 155, 158 (bottom), 196 (top): Erica Schlueter; pp. 4 (WHi-9566), 100 (WHi-1969), 136 (WHi-10983): Wisconsin Historical Society; pp. 6, 9, 11, 31, 38, 45 (Doug Alft), 73, 105, (Gary Knowles), 138, 150 (Timothy Hursley), 165, 174, 181, 195 (R. J. and Linda Miller), 197, 199, 203, 214, 227: Wisconsin Department of Tourism; p. 20: courtesy Bill Goulet; p. 27: courtesy *Burnett County Sentinel;* p. 40: Patti Brown, DNR; pp. 47, 158 (top): Jim Legault; p. 50: Trish Kempkes; p. 56: George Sroda; p. 65: courtesy Steven G. Krubsack; p. 77: Anton Rajer; p. 79: Clyde Wynia; p. 102: courtesy John Michael Kohler Arts Center; p. 121: Mark Madsen; p. 130: Rick Serocki; p. 143: courtesy KF Holdings, Inc.; p. 144: Jim Wildeman; p. 163: Skot Weidemann; p. 168: Joseph Blough; p. 180: courtesy Perfect Impressions; p. 189: courtesy International Crane Foundation; p. 193: courtesy Fennimore Cheese; pp. 196 (bottom), 201, 229: Jerry Minnich; p. 207: Kerri Marshall-Edgerly Photos; p. 211: courtesy City Brewery; p. 218: Jan Mangin; p. 232: courtesy Boaz Area Lions Club; p. 235: courtesy Carol Anderson. All other photographs by Diana Cook.

"Poniatowski" words and music by Peter Berryman © 1988 L & P Berryman

ISSN 1549-5094
ISBN 0-7627-3040-4

Manufactured in the United States of America
Second Edition/First Printing

CONTENTS

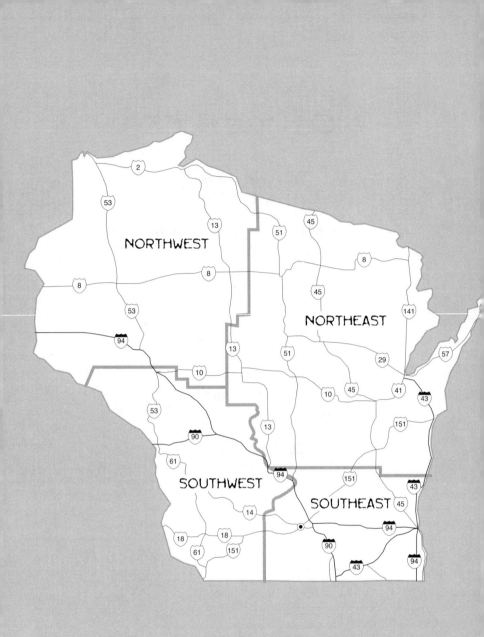

ACKNOWLEDGMENTS

I t was a pleasure to encounter many helpful people throughout Wisconsin in the course of this search for the unique, the unlikely, the delightfully strange, and the positively odd. These fine people include:

People with cameras who know how to use them. Erica Schlueter was a fine photographer, an artist with a keen eye for surprises along the road, and a navigator with solid map-reading skills. Jerry Minnich, who has been around the state a few times for his own books, provided car, camera, and counsel. Andy Kraushaar anticipated this project by long ago photographing just what the book needed. He then generously shared his work. Jim Legault was the same way.

People who know the territory or know someone who does. For instance, although Barb at the Iron River tourism office hadn't heard about the giant twine ball, she thought Bev at the historical museum 2 blocks over might know. Bev was not familiar with the twine ball but she knew who would be, Joe at the retirement center in Lake Nebagamon. And sure enough, Joe knew exactly where it was, and he didn't mind taking the time to locate the spot on the road map, even at the risk of missing a historic baseball moment on TV. . . These are our people.

Special thanks to the Wisconsin Department of Tourism, particularly Scott Thom in the film office, for providing photographs, and Mary Ellen Ruesch, who knows what's what and who to call. The folks at Wisconsin Tourism will help you, too. Call (800) 432–TRIP or check out the Web site at www.travelwisconsin.com.

We love to fish.

INTRODUCTION

Wisconsin is pretty much the way things should be. If you want woods, you go up north; for the Great Lakes, head east. The majestic Mississippi River configures our western boundary. And if for any reason you want to go to Illinois, simply point yourself south. But make sure to bring lots of change for the tolls, and remember that you can quickly return to our free and well-maintained highways for safaris to the interior of the Badger State.

Already blessed simply by being a native of Wisconsin (and don't kid yourself, it gives you a leg up on the wheeler-dealers from either coast), I was doubly lucky in having a father, David A., who believed that vacations should be educational. Broadly interpreted, that meant that visiting the world's largest fiberglass muskellunge (in Hayward) could be considered a learning experience.

Dad thought that it was important for kids to step on board the submarine in Manitowoc, to stumble across Al Capone's hideaway in the Northwoods, and to realize what one man carrying bricks on his back up a mountain (only slightly more ambitious than some of Dad's home projects) could build—namely, the cantilevered House on the Rock, made specifically to house the world's largest calliope collection (now a destination of its own in Spring Green). The Wisconsin Dells was our Amazon, the Chippewa Flowage our bayou, the Apostle Islands our Caribbean. Door County was our Cape Cod (even better, since there is no Packer Hall of Fame anywhere near Nantucket), Little Norway our Big Norway, and it's a fact that there are more miles of sand-duned beaches between Marinette and Kenosha than on the entire Côte d'Azur. And as Dad liked to say, it's a lot more convenient.

We would make forays all around the state. Dad was perhaps the first CPA to visit many of the villages where whitefish cheeks were a delicacy, as well as the endless number of fishing lakes where bass (the largemouth variety, not Abe Bass, our dear uncle in scrap metal) leaped into the boat, attracted by the cigar smoke. (Dad never actually did fish; he just sat in the boat smoking his cigar, safe in the knowledge that Mother was hundreds of miles away from smelling it.)

We hunkered down into cabins shaped like cement tepees, along main streets that still looked like Swedish frontier towns except for (or perhaps because of) the chainsaw-carved trolls lining the streets (Mount Horeb). We wandered onto reservations and through national forests. We were transported back in time to Belgian, Norwegian, German, Finnish, Cornish, and French towns founded by people trying to cover up the fact that they had emigrated. We ate our way through the diverse

Billboard on Highway 35 south of Hudson.

ethnic neighborhoods of Milwaukee, Racine, and Kenosha, and along the many stops of the Frank Lloyd Wright trail of beautiful land-hugging designs and leaky roofs.

If Dad is the inspiration, Diana Cook is the real heroine of this volume, having crisscrossed Wisconsin's Class B highways in search of elusive cat-whisker collections and cows with portholes in their stomachs (just one of the many options you can get with your cow in Wisconsin). Her travels have not been without reward. Along the way she teamed with a rural mail carrier to win the mixed doubles Seed-Spitting Championship at the Pardeeville Watermelon Festival, and for her efforts she now has a trophy—presented by Alice in Dairyland—resembling the Stanley Cup. She deserves that and more for her delightful investigative work deep into the heart of Dairyland.

I myself participated in the Prairie du Sac Cow Chip Throw one year, but I didn't even place. The old-timers say the trick is finding the cow chip with just the right moisture content, but I think some of the guys just know which Holstein to back.

We hope you'll find this guide to Wisconsin curiosities both fun and, as my father would maintain, educational, and that it will inspire you to pack up the Taurus wagon and explore our beautiful state. And if you find something a little bit out of the ordinary that we didn't, let us know—Wisconsin surely has many more secrets yet to reveal.

MICHAEL FELDMAN

Her real name is "Wisconsin," but everybody likes to call her "Ms. Forward,"
because she represents the state motto, "Forward." She has a "W" on her
chest, an ear of corn behind each ear, and a badger on her head. She left the
ground in July 1914 and has been perched atop the capitol dome in Madison
ever since. The badger's rear end is the highest point in Madison.

HOW TO TELL WISCONSIN FROM MINNESOTA

None of the curiosities described in this book will do you any good if you go looking for them in Minnesota, but due to what seems to be universal confusion or a muddying of our border waters, many of you may well do that. Don't. It would be a mistake. Minnesota already gets all the attention, what with Jesse Ventura and Garrison "the shy guy" Keillor. But Wisconsin is really where it's at, which is, facing the map with your nose pressed to the Mississippi River, on the right. True, Minnesotans and Wisconsinites are pretty similar. They're probably even close enough genetically to mate, although you'd be taking a chance. Maybe they're too close to mate. They claim 10,000 lakes, but we have at least that many that we don't even talk about because in Wisconsin, we think things speak for themselves, so we don't have to.

Wisconsinites and Minnesotans share a common heritage, having been overrun by the French, who loved us only for our furs; then by Scandinavians looking for a fjord to ford and Germans who couldn't cross a creek without wondering what kind of beer it would make. Neither of us are strangers to biting flies, Lutheran circles, garage art, covered dishes, Native American casinos, bingo in the church basement, lawn edging, and what outsiders might take for an unseemly interest in bovine growth and reproduction. We both keep herring in the house, and we both know that lefse is to be held like a cigar and that lutefisk and head cheese are not for the faint of heart. Yahtzee, euchre, and sheepshead will get you through a long winter night in either place as long as there's a brewski and a bowl of cheese curds for sustenance. Sturdy European stock furnished us both, although we in Wisconsin have been stereo-

typed as being the larger, when, in fact, we are simply big-
boned, with the accompanying nice personalities. They say in
Minnesota that when offered something, you refuse three times
before accepting; in Wisconsin I've seen it run up to six or
seven offers, depending upon what it is.

To the contiguous forty-six states, Minnesota and Wisconsin
overlap: People are always calling Kirby Puckett the unofficial
mayor of Milwaukee, or tagging Fred MacMurray as the pride
of St. Olaf's, much to the chagrin of the alumni of Carroll College in Waukesha, Wisconsin. Historically, the confusion stems
from the great tree steal of 1846, when the lumber barons
pulled Wisconsin's rug out from under the plat where Minneapolis and St. Paul now stand and lopped off the upper

Lucinda wannabes. A Marathon County Holstein named
Lucinda holds the world record for milk production. Her total of 67,914
pounds in one year averages out to twenty-two gallons of milk a day, four
times more than the average cow. She lives at Floyd and Lloyd Baumann's
Twin-B Dairy Farm near Marathon.

peninsula (currently of Michigan) like a giant appendix. Had they not been wrested from us, the Twin Cities would still be Pig's Eye and St. Anthony's Falls and suburbs of Hudson, Wisconsin, where Cray Super Computers got their start despite Minnesota's claim to be "The Brainpower State" (with billboards on the border facing us!).

Why then, given the commonalities, the shared history and heritage, and the fact that nobody can tell us apart, do we in God's Country (technically just La Crosse, but why confine Him?) continue to feel like Roger Clinton or a pillow stuffed with unknown fiber? Are we the former East Germany to Minnesota's former West? Why do we feel inferior even though some of us are living in Superior? Are the citizens of Minnesota's Lake Wobegon more perfect?

Perhaps it's just a difference in style. For example, the dual burghers of Kenosha/Racine, Neenah/Menasha, and Sauk City/ Prairie du Sac, Wisconsin, would never dream of referring to themselves as "The Cities," as residents of Minneapolis/St. Paul do. We know for a fact that there are others, including the Quad Cities (which, with two pair, win). Maybe it's the Cheesehead thing, which only recently occurred to us to be an insult, depending on who says it. Maybe it's just the way Minnesotans stand out like sore thumbs when they cross over in their painfully coordinated colors with names like periwinkle and sage, and in parkas that look like they've never been worn, let alone to change the oil. Fording the St. Croix is not exactly crossing the Uatuma in Brazil. But in the interests of peace in the neighborhood and upholding the sovereignty of the great state of Wisconsin, here are ten ways to tell that you're in Wisconsin and not Minnesota:

1. People are driving 55 mph in the passing lane. It's well within our rights; after all, the minimum is 40, so we're actually speeding. They raised it to 65 in spots, but that's not our problem. Unlike those fleeing Minnesota to their cabins in Wisconsin, we're in no hurry to get anywhere. Plus, hit a deer at 55 and chances are good that one or both of you will walk away.

2. Speaking of cabins, you know that you're in Wisconsin if
    you see an SUV with Brainerd (MN) plates backing up a
    bass boat to the lake. What with only 10,000 lakes (many
    scarcely more than puddles) and an average of 100 cabin
    sites per, there are only 1 million indigenous cabins for
    4 million Minnesotans—a shortfall of some 30,000 lakes
    that they're not going to find in landlocked Iowa.

3. We don't brag about our children's SAT scores in Wisconsin,
    and not because they don't have them. While Minnesotans
    may edge us out in some tests, you tell me who the Min-
    nesota Multiphasic Personality Inventory is geared toward.

4. If it's "Come as you are," it's Wisconsin. The knockoff Ital-
    ian double-breasteds and off-the-shoulder cocktail dresses
    favored in some places don't cut it here. While the state
    motto is "Forward," it may as well be "Whatever's Clean."
    When we say "Dress," we mean "Wear clothes."

5. If people don't go outdoors in winter, you're in the Twin
    Cities, scurrying through the skyways like gerbils in a
    maze. Cold doesn't faze us here—that's why we even bother
    to ask, "Cold enough for you?" It's not meant to be ironic. If
    we don't get out in the cold, our winter coats dull and we
    start to shed. If you need skyways, Madison has as fine a
    web of steam tunnels as you could hope for, and Milwaukee
    is the Venice of alleys. Up north you can always find a
    snowmobile trail and flag somebody down.

6. If you're halfway between the equator and the North Pole
    and a quarter of the way around the world from Green-
    wich, England, you're in the capital of the northwestern
    world: Poniatowski, Wisconsin. This is just one example of
    how unexpected Wisconsin can be—from the world's largest
    ginseng fields in Marathon County to the rumored site of
    the Garden of Eden in Galesville (where, when Adam and
    Eve were expelled from Paradise, they went to Minnesota).
    This book is filled with things that you are simply not
    going to find in Minnesota: the world's largest talking cow,

The Infinity Room at House on the Rock.

in Neillsville; the largest loon, in Mercer; the largest six-pack, in La Crosse; the largest *M,* in Platteville (which at 400 tons would crush any letter in the Hollywood Hills); and the four-and-a-half-story muskie, in Hayward, from whose jaws, if your wife gets down low enough to take the picture, you can appear to be dangling. Two can play at this "world-class" game.

7. If you show up with your spouse and no one else at a restaurant or coffee shop and the girl asks you "How many?" you're in Wisconsin. We take nothing for granted. If you insist on waiting for a booth, don't block the cigarette machine. Don't ask to see the menu before you sit down—it's not going to change things any, and the waitstaff resents it. If you're here on business, please remember

that we don't "take a lunch" in Wisconsin, we eat one, and we'll be happy to chat after the fried ice cream.

8. "Uff da!" and similar Norwegian exclamations occur in both states, but clearly Wisconsin is where a water fountain is a "bubbler" and "Ain'a hey" is the equivalent of "Mon Dieu!" If possible, begin all stories with "So I says . . .," and make sure it's one worth telling: We have very high standards.

9. Wisconsin, the Côte d'Azur of the upper Midwest, averages 2 to 4 degrees Fahrenheit warmer than Minnesota, and 360 degrees warmer than the dark side of Mercury (not counting wind chill), so pack accordingly.

10. You may be able to find a pair of fish cheeks in the land of the Golden Gopher, but fish boils come from Door County,

Larry Primeau of De Pere mounted a deer rack to a 1960s Packer helmet and became the Green Bay Packalope. Green and gold Mardi Gras beads (recalling the Super Bowl XXXI victory in New Orleans) and a mini-cheese wedge complete his ensemble. He represents the Packers in the Visa Hall of Fans, but he's still number 3,500 on the waiting list for season tickets.

Wisconsin, a fact that so many Minnesotans and others are aware of, it's getting impossible to get into one. So you might just want to head out to the deck with a large kettle, half a face cord of oak, a dozen small red potatoes, one-and-a-half pounds of small onions, a cheesecloth, eight quarts of water, a pound of salt, two or three pounds of fish steaks, one cup of butter, a pile of lemon wedges, and a couple of quarts of kerosene, and take things into your own hands. Since this is a potentially fatal combination, however, feel free to call and we'll talk you down—or, better yet, come by the house and we'll head for the White Gull.

A 16-foot, one-ton loon emphasizes Mercer's claim as the Loon Capital.

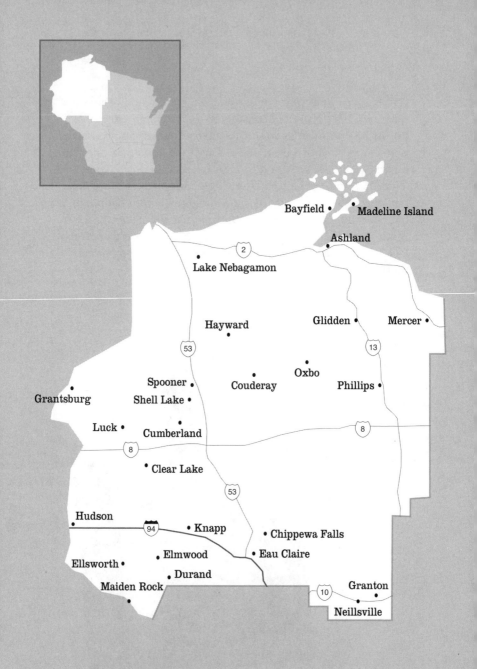

Bayfield •
Madeline Island •

Ashland •

Lake Nebagamon •

Glidden •
Mercer •

Hayward •

Oxbo •

Spooner •
Couderay •
Phillips •

Grantsburg •
Shell Lake •

Luck •
Cumberland •

Clear Lake •

Hudson •
Knapp •
Chippewa Falls •

Ellsworth •
Elmwood •
Eau Claire •

Durand •
Granton •

Maiden Rock •
Neillsville •

NORTHWEST

NORTHWEST

The northwest section of Wisconsin is extremely watery. Not only is it bounded on the north by Lake Superior and on the west by the St. Croix and the Mississippi Rivers (except for a 40-mile stretch where Minnesotans and Wisconsinites could, if they chose, stand cheek to jowl), but it has zillions of lakes and rivers. In summer you will notice that many people have fishing poles on their shoulders or canoes on their heads. In winter, when all the water is frozen, they continue fishing by drilling holes in the ice.

This part of Wisconsin is also very woodsy. The Chequamegon-Nicolet National Forest alone covers a million and a half acres (and includes 600 of those lakes). On a Saturday in February, thousands of cross-country skiers from all over the world race through the woods from Hayward to Cable in the 51K Birkebeiner, the largest cross-country ski marathon in North America. They recall the birkebeiner skiers who, in the year 1206, skied through the rugged forests of Norway to smuggle the illegitimate son of King Sverresson and Inga of Vartieg to safety. Today's skiers wear spandex instead of birkebeiners (birchbark leggings), but they have the same desperate and determined look in their eyes.

The rest of the year, people of the northwest apply the same kind of intensity to less spectacular pursuits, such as taxidermy, string collecting, and tick racing. Peering down the gravel spurs that branch off from the secondary roads, you wonder what other passions and obsessions the woods conceal.

The most populous place in the northwest section of Wisconsin is the city of Eau Claire, with 61,000 people. But for the most part, there is more space where no one is than where someone is, and that is what makes the northwest what it is.

RUNNING THEM RAGGEDY
Bayfield

Irene and Richard Radke have been living among thousands of smiling faces of Raggedy Ann and Andy—not only the dolls but also their images on music boxes, dishes, furniture, clothing, costumes, planters, snow globes, cookie jars, banks, bedding, radios, towels, nightlights, cookie molds, canned goods, piñatas . . . A look around convinces you in a matter of seconds how lucky Irene and Richard were to find each other. Luckier, if they still *can* amid all the Raggedys.

The Radkes' collection fills the house from top to bottom. The Raggedys and their paraphernalia cover the chairs, couches, tables, and shelves of the living and dining areas. Upstairs (a doll is perched on every step along the way) they occupy all the key bathroom fixtures and presumably use the products at hand—the Raggedy toothbrushes, dispensers, soap, nail polish, and makeup kits. They sit at little desks in the schoolroom, and they nap in little cradles in the day-care center. They monopolize the beds and store their notepaper, greeting cards, Christmas ornaments, and such in all the dresser drawers. Their linens and clothing cram the closets.

Among the posters and art that have been framed is a cartoon in which Raggedy Ann—huggable and homespun, button-eyed and slue-footed—watches a Barbie doll trying on a new outfit. "You're so lucky you can wear anything," she says. "I wonder if that comes in half sizes?"

The collection began more than thirty years ago when Irene, her mother, and her son all happened to select Raggedy Ann music boxes as gifts for the Radkes' newborn daughter. It was a sign from above to go all out, until the Radkes had the largest collection anywhere.

A bright-eyed class of Raggedy scholars.

Last year, however, the Radkes began to wonder about life outside Raggedyland. Lovable as they are, the Raggedys and all their stuff were tying them down. So, much as they hated to do it, they decided to sell their house, collection and all, and make plans to see the world through their own eyes—not shoe-button ones. Unless all those Raggedys got out their magic Wishing Pebbles, the Radkes might be on their way by now.

Wood from When the Earth Was Young

Diving in the chilly depths of Chequamegon Bay, in Lake Superior off Ashland, is a bit like peering through a telescope pointed at the far end of the galaxy: You can see things that no longer exist. In this neck of the woods, that means submerged logs from the primeval forests of Wisconsin—slow-growth oak, cherry, maple, birch, elm, bird's-eye maple—perfectly preserved by the frigid, low-oxygen waters. These tens or perhaps hundreds of thousands of logs are what remain of virgin forests cut and floated to mills long gone; in the 1870s and 1880s, these were the stands felled to rebuild burned-out Chicago.

This was timber already old when it was cut more than a hundred years ago—350-year-old maple, for example, of a quality no longer seen anywhere, except perhaps in a Stradivarius. (In fact, some of the interest in the maple "sinkers" comes from instrument makers hoping to duplicate violins with wood very much like that which the master used; if Stradivari himself is preserved down there, they may have some luck.)

Timeless Timber, a company that hoped to retrieve 20,000 to 30,000 logs a year from the bay, suffered a setback when the Red Cliff band of the Lake Superior Chippewa objected to their removal under nineteenth-century treaties; all future reclamation will be done with the cooperation of the tribe and the Army Corps of Engineers. But after all, the forest primeval has waited this long—it can wait a little bit longer.

THE DIFFERENCE IS, GAYLORD NELSON COULDN'T THROW A SPITTER TO SAVE HIS LIFE
Clear Lake

The Clear Lake Museum proudly—and somewhat incongruously—presents Burleigh Grimes and Gaylord Nelson, two sons of Clear Lake who made good.

Grimes grew up on a farm nearby, walked to school across Clear Lake during the winter, played on the Clear Lake Red Jackets, and ended up in the Baseball Hall of Fame as one of the great spitball pitchers. In fact, he was the last pitcher to throw legal spitballs (balls that have been spat upon or somehow moistened to make them break more sharply). Baseball outlawed them in 1920 but exempted the seventeen pitchers in the major leagues who depended on them for their livelihood, such as Grimes. "Ol' Stubblebeard" (he didn't shave on days he pitched) outlasted them all, frightening hitters until 1934. "[Grimes] walked with a swagger that infuriated batters, and when he measured a hitter from the mound he would peel back his lips to show yellow teeth in a snarl," wrote the *New York Times* in his obituary in 1985.

Among a great deal of memorabilia are his St. Louis Cardinals and New York Yankees uniforms, a baseball autographed by Herbert Hoover, and his personal license plate, BAG 270 (Burleigh Arland Grimes, 270 winning games).

A sportswriter once said, "Let's see, Mr. Grimes, you were from a small town up in Northern Wisconsin, Clear Lake?" Replied Grimes, "If you were good enough, you were from Clear Lake."

Gaylord Nelson was good enough to become governor of Wisconsin (1959–63) and U.S. senator (1963–81), and to earn a

spotless reputation in both public and private life. The son of a
local doctor, he grew up exploring the wilderness at the end of
Clear Lake's Main Street. He took his love of Wisconsin's great
outdoors to Washington, sponsored environmental legislation,
and founded Earth Day. President Clinton thanked him with
the Presidential Medal of Freedom, and in 1999 the National
Audubon Society named him and Theodore Roosevelt the two
most influential environmentalists of the twentieth century.
The museum focuses on his career and includes some childhood items.

Of each of them, curator Charles Clark says, "You couldn't
meet a nicer guy." The museum is at 450 Fifth Avenue. Hours
are irregular. For information call Mr. Clark at (715) 263–2042.

WHEN THE BEARS PAID
FOR PROTECTION
Couderay

Al Capone was nothing if not diversified. Bootlegging, gam-
bling, vice, racketeering, bumping off guys, fishing. If he
had only paid his taxes, he might be here today, in his 500-acre
retreat in the cool and stately pine-and-hardwood forest near
Couderay. The wily traveler can find it by following the neon
sign that says AL CAPONE'S HIDEOUT. In his day, however, this
Northwoods pied-à-terre was so low-profile that even Mrs.
Capone didn't know about it. Of course, she may have been
the last to know.

To make sure that no one disturbed his peace and quiet and
fishing, Capone built a gun tower—unusual in the Northwoods
at the time—as well as outbuildings with walls 18 inches thick,
and a jail cell for unwelcome visitors. Little did the local trades-

men and craftsmen who hauled all that fieldstone in the 1920s know who they were working for. Or so they said.

In 1931 "Public Enemy Number One" had to hang up his fishing pole and head for prison for income-tax evasion—not as colorful a rap as some others that the feds might have pinned on him, but sufficient to keep him off the streets for the next eight years.

Guided tours include the grounds and the main lodge with its spiral staircases, deer-horn fixtures, and slightly salacious mannequins perched on the beds. The garage (with four built-in gun portholes) that used to house long black limousines is now a restaurant and bar.

Really well hidden. From Hayward take Highway B to NN to N to CC . . . et cetera (23 miles). Or, from Highway 70 at Couderay, go north on Highway CC (6 miles). Tours from noon to 6:00 P.M. daily, Memorial Day through Labor Day; noon to 5:00 P.M. for three-day weekends through October. Admission charge. For more information call (715) 945–2746.

The village of Luck was once the yo-yo capital of the world. In the 1950s and '60s the Duncan plant in Luck used the area's hard maple trees to produce millions of yo-yos.

THE RUTABAGA-FREE FESTIVAL
Cumberland

They've taken the rutabaga out of the Rutabaga Festival. The bland and homely root vegetable—something like a cross between a cabbage and a turnip—is no longer the big cash crop that it was in these parts when the festival started,

This 1940s red Farmall H tractor is no ordinary tractor-on-a-post. It rotates, and at night its lights sweep across the sky. The handy landmark is at 8892 Highway 178 near Chippewa Falls. Its creator, Bill Goulet, says it also makes a good birdhouse.

back in 1932. Gone are the days of the rutabaga bakeoff and the rutabaga cookbook. And if they talk about them at all, they call them "baggies." Even the festival queen is crowned "Miss Cumberland," not "Miss Rutabaga."

You can take the rutabaga out of the festival, but you can't take the festival out of Cumberland. The festivities carry on for four days over the weekend before Labor Day, with a parade, live music, a hot-pepper-eating contest, a pancake breakfast, and an ice-cream social. But nary a nod to the humble rutabaga.

The Chamber of Commerce sponsors the Rutabaga Festival. Call (715) 822-3378 for more information.

The nearby town of Boyceville also celebrates a phantom vegetable. Although the pickle factory left a few years ago, the Cucumber Festival goes on, at least in name. A grand parade, a souped-up garden-tractor pull, and other events take the place of the treasure hunt for the Golden Cucumber or the Cucumber Float down the creek. The festival is held during the third week in August. Call (715) 643-2298 for more information.

The bumper stickers read REAL TOURISTS EAT WHITEFISH LIVERS because Bayfield discovered that if you stop calling them fish guts, you can sell them to tourists as a real delicacy. Restaurants sauté them in butter, sometimes combined with red peppers and onions or with bacon, onion, and mushrooms. The Norwegian way is to stew them in milk. ("They like to have all their food white," explains one chef.) Gourmet shops sell them pureed in a pâté. Local fish markets sell them straight, for those who want to rustle up a batch at home.

RUN BAMBI, RUN!
Durand

Anna Mae Bauer has had eighteen collisions with deer on the road. "It's not as if I'm out to set a record or anything," says Anna Mae, who probably *has* set a record.

Nevertheless, the intrepid Anna Mae continues to drive nearly 500 miles a week between her home in Durand and her job in Chippewa Falls. Traveling a heavily wooded highway somewhat increases the odds here.

Not all the deer were killed on the spot. Number One (sometime in 1958) was just dazed a little; others have been able to stumble away into the woods.

As a regular customer, Anna Mae now consults the guys at G&W Body Shop in Durand before buying a new car, anticipating the need to match paint and so on. And she has high praise for her insurance company, though on occasion she's been too embarrassed to file yet another claim.

For a while she had four or five deer alerts attached to the front of her car. They were supposed to warn deer of her approach, but the animals leaped into her path anyway—and took the devices with them as they went down. Anna Mae does not invest in deer alerts anymore.

Deer Number Seventeen (December 19, 1998) had a curious response. As Anna Mae got out of the car and approached, the deer raised its head and gazed at her, as if to say, "You must be the Anna Mae Bauer I've heard so much about," then lay down and died.

The Wisconsin Department of Natural Resources reports that almost 45,000 deer were killed by vehicles in one recent year—not all driven by Anna Mae Bauer. (If you're coming this way, the locals advise keeping the windows rolled down so the deer can jump right through.)

MILK

*O*ne day back in the 1980s, Governor Lee Dreyfus liked the cheese curds he sampled in Ellsworth so much that he proclaimed the town to be the "Cheese Curds Capital." The cheesemakers of Ellsworth are modest about this honor, saying that no one really makes cheese curds, they're just scraps left over from an early stage of the cheddar-making process.

Ellsworth produces millions of pounds of cheese curds each year. They are not aged—the flavor "hasn't built up to a crescendo," a fact unrelated to the noise they make when eaten. Some people think cheese curds are peculiar, as if eating bland little lumps that squeak is something to snicker at.

YOU'RE CLEARED FOR LANDING
Elmwood

Thousands of Earthlings, some in costume, come to Elmwood, population 775, for UFO Days in July.

The first reported sighting of a UFO here occurred in March 1975. Something like a very bright star chased a mother and her three children home and tried to land in front of their car. A few nights later police officer George Wheeler sighted "a flaming ball the size of a football field." It zapped his car with a blue light that burned out all the plugs and points. The CIA investigated. Even Dan Rather came.

Enough sightings occurred over the next several years that in 1988 Elmwood announced plans for a $25 million visitor center—for aliens. It would include a gigantic beacon and landing strip, a huge image on the ground to welcome space travelers, accommodations and laboratories for dozens of scientists, and a video studio. "This is not a gimmick," said the mayor.

The ground image caused considerable debate. The sketch from a local artist showed two lanky figures shaking hands. What if a handshake doesn't mean the same thing to aliens that it means to humans? "If they're smart enough to get here," said the mayor, "they're smart enough to figure everything else out." The handshake stayed.

Elmwood dropped the plan for the visitor center for lack of funds, but it has an annual celebration on the last full weekend in July. There's a parade, dancing, horseshoe and cow-chip throwing, and of course UFO burgers, buttons, and bumper stickers. Call (715) 639–3792 for more information.

ALL DRESSED OUT AND NOWHERE TO GO
Glidden

Here lies the "World Record Black Bear." It was killed 5 miles northeast of Glidden on November 23, 1963.

Hjalmer Krans had noticed a bear den while looking over a timber tract in a cedar swamp and reported his discovery to two hunters, Otto Hedbany and Donald Streubel of New Berlin. According to the *Glidden Enterprise*, "The bear had been

Yet another feather in Wisconsin's cap: the World's Largest Pine Log.

denned for some time and did not bestir itself when discovered. Mr. Hedbany had no difficulty in killing the animal with one shot in the head, fired from his 303 Savage rifle. It took seven men about an hour to drag the bear 150 yards to a car."

The hunters weighed the bear at the Schraufnagel Lumber Yard: 665 pounds "dressed out." It measured 7 feet 10 inches from tail to nose and 72 inches around the chest, and it was estimated to be twelve years old.

The bear is on display in a glass-and-log case next to the world's largest white pine log (1,940 board feet). It is 2 blocks east of Highway 13, just off Grant Street.

PAUL BUNYAN JUST GOT BETTER PRESS
Grantsburg

A life-size wood sculpture of a hometown hero, Anders Gustav Anderson (1872–1926), stands in front of the village office at 416 South Pine Street. "Big Gust" stood a well-proportioned 7 feet 6 inches (that's 4 inches taller than Kareem Abdul-Jabbar), weighed 360 pounds, and wore size eighteen shoes (Kareem's are size sixteen).

Born in Sweden, Big Gust was village marshal of Grantsburg for the last twenty-five years of his life and the biggest police officer in the country. According to one story, Gust once broke up a disturbance at the local saloon by hoisting a man under each arm and heading toward the jail. At Oak and Madison they asked to be put down and walked peaceably the rest of the way. He was also helpful if power lines needed to be strung or if a car or even a house needed to be lifted, for he was very strong.

Gust was also good-natured. When he died no one could recall an angry or unkind word from him; and if there were, chances are they would have let it pass.

*Grantsburg didn't have
a basketball team.*

Alf Manley Olson, a lifelong resident of Grantsburg, carved
the Big Gust likeness in 1980 from laminated basswood. It
weighs eight pounds more than Gust did. The Grantsburg Area
Historical Society Museum, located at 133 West Wisconsin
Avenue, displays the crutch specially built for Gust when he
slipped on ice in front of the fire hall in 1918 and broke his
hip, along with other items that indicate his size.

Grantsburg celebrates Big Gust Days the first weekend of
June each year.

WHAT'S TALL, HAIRY, AND DOESN'T WEAR A FAVRE JERSEY?

*A*lthough Sasquatch—Bigfoot, to his friends—is most often associated with the Pacific Northwest, someone forgot to tell James Hughes of Granton, a deliveryman for the Black River Shopper. While on his route on County Highway H at about 5:15 on the morning of March 28, 2000, Hughes saw a hirsute, ape-faced creature a good 8 feet tall and easily 500 pounds making off with a goat under one arm. Since the thing still had one arm free, Hughes put the pedal to the metal and left the Shoppers in his trunk. In his report to the Clark County Sheriff's Department, he described the beast as "all covered with hair, a real dark gray color, with some spots that look a honey color. It was walking on two legs, and it was mighty, mighty, big." Hughes feared for his life, but the creature had already gotten his goat. The sheriff, unable to find any footprints or scat, said he had no reports of goats missing, let alone, well, you know.

According to the Milwaukee Journal Sentinel, Hughes waited a day to file his report, fearing that people would think him crazy, but stressed,

"I don't drink, I don't use dope, and I was wide awake."

It would be easy to dismiss this report as an aberration were it not for the fact that Bigfoot sightings in Wisconsin have been numerous, dating from at least to 1910, when a large, hairy creature followed a ten-year-old girl home, leaving tracks "twice as large as her father's." Before that a similar beast, the Windigo, was known to the Chippewa and incorporated into their tribal lore. In The W-Files, *author Jay Rath recounts sightings of huge, upright, animal-like creatures in Delavan in 1964; in Waupaca County in 1968 (where a group of hunters would have shot it had it only looked a little less human); in Lafayette County in 1970; and in 1992 in southeastern Wisconsin, standing over a roadkill on State Highway 106. More sightings of this last creature attracted national media, as well as tour buses from Illinois, and excited such alliterations as the Werewolf of Walworth County and* The Beast of Bray Road, *a book by Linda Godfrey.*

All the descriptions are much the same as Hughes's. Needless to say, to see something of that size in Wisconsin without so much as a shred of Packer paraphernalia on it can only be described as very, very curious indeed.

Granton is in Clark County, about 10 miles east of Neillsville.

FASTEST SHOW ON H_2O
Grantsburg

What's the fun of having a snowmobile if you can run around in it only about eight months out of the year? Some such thinking inspired the activity on Memory Lake that now attracts thousands of spectators every summer: drag races in snowmobiles on open water, something that usually happens only at bar time—Wisconsin parlance for closing time—when the ice is breaking up.

Three or four snowmobiles at a time take a 20-foot run from the shore, hit the water, and skip across the top, the way a rock skips across a pond. The fastest one wins—and speeds can reach 65 or 70 mph on the straightaway. Another event involves racing around a series of buoys. Whichever, unless it's done very fast, the snowmobile sinks.

To see it is to believe it. The World Championship Snowmobile Watercross takes place on the third weekend in July. Call (715) 463–5466 for information.

Dick's Bar in Hudson serves chicken in a hubcap with soup and salad on the side. Those who must know why are told of a dream involving chickens and hubcaps, "and if you understand that, we've failed." No need to count your hubcaps before you drive away.

Dick's has been in this location since 1860: next to the marina on the Mississippi River, 111 Walnut Street (old Highway 12). Open 8:00 A.M. to bar time. Give them a call at (715) 386–5222.

THERE'S ALWAYS A CATCH
Hayward

The Fresh Water Fishing Hall of Fame has hundreds of outboard motors from way back when ("Look! There's Grandpa's old motor!"), thousands of fishing poles and rods and reels, and more kinds of minnow buckets than you ever dreamed of. It's a trip down memory lane of tackle boxes and depth finders. It's also the last word on freshwater fishing records. If you think you have a trophy, have it authenticated here.

The de rigueur photo op of your trip to northern Wisconsin, for not just you but up to twenty or thirty of your traveling companions—that's how big the jaws of this muskie are at the Fishing Hall of Fame. Big enough for weddings.

But the part that made our hearts beat faster was the exhibit of hundreds of fishing hooks and lures that have snagged fishermen, each one documented by the angler's name, hometown (Illinois is well represented), and year and lake of snag. It began with the collection of a Grantsburg doctor who started to save the hooks and lures sticking out of people who turned up at his office about once a week for thirty-eight summers. It didn't even have to be summertime; some people hooked themselves cleaning out their tackle boxes in the middle of winter. Other doctors have joined in the fun to build the impressive collection on display here.

Also noteworthy is the wall of "Poor Taxidermy," the pathetic attempts of amateurs that resulted in misshapen fish or mounts that deteriorated from the use of inferior materials. With all the taxidermists in business in the Northwoods, there's really no need to try this at home.

Did we mention that all these wonders are housed in a 4-and-a-half-story, ½-block-long, walk-through fiberglass muskie?

The National Fresh Water Fishing Hall of Fame is at the junction of Highways 27 and B. Open daily 10:00 A.M. to 4:30 P.M. (to 5:00 P.M. in the summer), April 15 to November 1. For more information see the Web site at www.freshwater-fishing .org, or call (715) 634–4440.

PULL UP YOUR GALLUSES AND HEAD FOR THE TIMBER
Hayward

If you've always worn red Flannels and suspenders and searched in vain for like-minded individuals, you'll want to add to the cries of "Yo-ho!" at the Lumberjack World Championships. Lumberjacks and lumberjills come from all over the world to compete in such events as the springboard chop, hot saw, underhand chop, logrolling, boom run, and speed climb.

Muscular competitors climb up and down trees about 90 feet tall very, very fast. They saw through logs in a wink. They spin big logs underfoot while trying to dump each other into the water. They toss axes all over the place. In short, it's a lot like where you work, only outdoors. Today, of course, all these things are usually done by machine (the logroller can dump a guy in the drink in a split second), so it's a glimpse of life in the Northwoods in days gone by.

This big event, along with other activities and music, takes place on the last full weekend in July at Lumberjack Bowl, a quarter of a mile east of Hayward on Highway B. Call (715) 634–2484 for more information.

P.S. Galluses are suspenders.

To Taxidermy
Hayward

The trouble with most dead things is they don't make you laugh. But that is easily remedied in Hayward at the whimsical Moccasin Bar, which features better drinking through taxidermy.

We're talking more than your usual fetal deer tableau here. We're talking rabbits in calico kibitzing at sheepshead and Tyrolean-hatted chipmunks drinking beer and rolling dice. Things that would have been, had evolution favored rodents and other small mammals instead of us. See what might have been at this popular local hangout.

Folks come for the "World's Largest Muskie"—the world's largest *mounted* muskie, that is—alone, although larger ones have been caught since Cal Johnson fought for this one (67½

*Judge Wolf hears the case of the badger
that jumped the woodcock season at the
Moccasin Bar in Hayward.*

pounds and 60¼ inches) for an hour on July 24, 1949. Just a
few months later, for instance, Louis Spray caught a larger one
and had it mounted, too, but the trophy was lost when the real-
estate office where it hung burned down. So life giveth, and it
taketh away. The authenticator of records, the Fresh Water
Fishing Hall of Fame (p. 31), sorts it all out.

The Moccasin Bar is at the junction of Highways 63 and 27.
Open 9:00 A.M. to bar time daily. Call (715) 634–4211.

*H**untsinger Farms of Eau Claire is the world's
largest grower and processor of horseradish.*

AMERICA'S DIARYLAND

Jim Cummings, of Knapp, has written in his diary every day since January 1, 1952, when he was thirteen years old—hasn't missed a day in nearly half a century. Even on days when nothing has happened. And it's not just "Sunny, high of 80 degrees, washed the car," but about 800 words daily of activities, thoughts, and impressions.

"It's about the only way I know to honor time," he says. "Otherwise it's time past, chaos dimly remembered." It also serves as a reality check. Rereading entries reveals that things he thought he remembered well aren't necessarily so. Writing with a fountain pen in permanent blue-black ink, he fills large red leather-bound volumes that by the end of a year contain nearly 300,000 words.

A respected and lifelong book buyer and seller by profession, Jim Cummings also owns 16,000 published English-language diaries. He added a special diary room at his home in western Wisconsin for what is probably the most extensive such collection anywhere.

His own diary entries are distinct enough that reading what he wrote on a given day years ago puts him back in that day and prompts the recollection of further details. "It's interesting to be able to reclaim any day that I've lived. Diaries put you right exactly where you were, fix you in a point as nothing else can do," he says.

Knowing the past is not the only reward of such diligence. Keeping a diary reminds Jim to lead a life that's interesting to record.

MARK TWINE
Lake Nebagamon

Jim Kotera has a mighty big ball of twine. He started it in 1979, after reading about other twine balls around the country. There are quite a few of them, although nobody knows why. Maybe because they are less painful to collect than balls of barbed wire.

From the beginning Jim has kept track of the size of his ball—"I take a whole bunch of twine, put it in a garbage bag, and weigh the garbage bag"—and according to his records, the

Jim Kotera's twine ball.

twine ball now weighs 18,200 pounds. That's assuming a twine ball wound weighs the same as a twine ball unwound. Along the way he's marked it on door jambs like a toddler. Today it's all growed up: 7 feet tall, 35 feet across, and potato shaped, since Jim has to work the angles now that it's too big to roll.

If Jim Kotera's calculations are correct (and unless someone has a ten-ton twine ball hidden away somewhere), he has the largest twine ball assembled by one man. There's one in Darwin, Minnesota, but it weighs a mere 17,400 pounds and measures 12 feet (Darwinians nevertheless hold an annual festival called Twine Ball Days in August). And there's one that Ripley's Believe It or Not Museum in Branson, Missouri, flaunts as Guinness-record-size, but it was a group effort, as was the 11-footer in Cawker City, Kansas (which calls its August celebration Twine-a-thon).

A farmer in the neighborhood has supplied much of the twine, and now he can't find anything to bundle his papers with. Meanwhile Jim built a pole shed over the ball for protection from winter weather. It's located at 8009 Oakdale Road (at Minnesong Road), Town of Highland, near Lake Nebagamon. Once you find the Oakdale Road–Minnesong Road intersection, it will be the giant potato-shaped twine ball on the left. Call (715) 374-3518 for more information.

IN A BLIZZARD, OF COURSE, YOU COULD ACTUALLY BE DRIVING UP CHRISTMAS TREES
Madeline Island

Highway H in Bayfield County is 2½ miles longer in winter than the rest of the year. That's because it extends to Madeline Island from Bayfield when Chequamegon Bay freezes

*The Nelson brothers' windsled transports schoolchildren,
commuters, groceries, and library books.*

over—usually in January. Regular ferry service ends, and
all kinds of other transportation begin. Say you live on the
island and want to get to Bayfield; you have your choice of
snowmobile, van, car, or windsled (a vehicle that combines boat,
plane, and sled). Or, if you want to know what it would be like
to live on Mars, you could walk. Your choice depends on the
condition of the ice.

Your route is a road of ice that is plowed, outlined in
Christmas trees, and maintained until the ice starts to thaw,
usually in March or April. Car-shaped holes in the ice indicate
that the ice-road season is over. *Whatever you do, don't go out
on that ice without first calling Arnie and Ronnie Nelson.* They
know the ice and have maintained the road for years.
Windsleds, Inc., (715) 747–5400.

MOVING IS NEVER EASY

*T*he old-timers had doubts about the wisdom of moving a house across the ice, but the movers (from Minneapolis) said they'd checked it—2 feet thick all the way across. The furnished seven-room, two-story house and trailer (twenty tons) were to be towed from Port Superior to Madeline Island on a truck (ten tons), a distance of slightly more than 3 miles. The ice-wise shook their heads.

On March 2, 1977, the thirty-ton cavalcade set out across the ice. Things went well most of the way, but then, just a mile from Madeline Island, the wheels under the house dropped through on one side, and the "Spectacle on Ice" came to a full halt. From the shore the gallery watched the house slowly settle into the water and disappear.

"The only thing sticking up was the chimney of the fireplace," recalls Ed Erickson, a veteran of these waters. "We filled the chimney with sandbags and that didn't go, so then we hauled rock and set rocks on the eaves, and it settled to the bottom of the lake."

In the spring Ed tried to lift the house, but it fell apart. He hauled up the pieces, but the floor is still down there.

WHERE THERE'S SMOKEY
Mercer

Until 1950 Smokey Bear existed only on paper—in posters and advertisements of the National Forest Service. But that was before the rangers at the station in Mercer needed an idea for a parade float for the Fireman's Convention in Hurley in August. Inspired by a recent Smokey Bear poster, their float featured a bearskin-and-wood Smokey praying under the sign AND PLEASE MAKE PEOPLE CAREFUL. AMEN.

The nation's first Smokey Bear
head is at the ranger station in Mercer.

Smokey reappeared the following month at the Logging Congress parade in Wausau, this time in the form of a ranger wearing a bear costume. Smokey Bear personified was a big hit!

The idea spread like wildfire, and before long the National Forest Service was suiting up lots of Smokeys. Today the Wisconsin Department of Natural Resources is officially credited with fabricating the first Smokey Bear costume.

The head of the original costume is at the Mercer area ranger station. Conservation aide Frank Brunner Jr. created it, and years later forestry technician Dave Sleight rescued it from a warehouse. A good collection of vintage posters is on display, too. The ranger station is half a mile north of town, on State House Road. Open 8:00 A.M. to 4:30 P.M. Monday and Friday or by appointment. Call (715) 476–2240 for more information.

S mokey Bear appears in the Fourth of July parade and at Mercer's annual Loon Day in August. (Well, actually, it's the official USDA Forest Service costume—in accordance with Smokey Bear Act of 1952, Public Law 82-359— containing a human and a NASA-worthy cooling system so Smokey doesn't pass out.) Loon Day includes loon-calling contests.

LARGEST TALKING COW AND CHEESE REPLICA
Neillsville

C hatty Belle is the world's largest talking cow, and the little guy standing next to her—but drop a quarter in the slot and let her tell the story: "Hi, so nice to see you. My name is Chatty Belle and beside me is my son, Bullet. Bullet doesn't talk yet but he's learning. What's your name? [pause] Well, nice to meet you. Did you know I'm the world's largest talking cow? I'm 16 feet high at the shoulders and 20 feet long, seven times as large as the average Holstein." Her voice seems high for such a large cow.

Largest cheese replica, that is.
Cheesemakers ate the real one at their
annual convention.

After reciting statistics of grain consumed and milk produced, Chatty Belle explains about the semi trailer parked next
to her. It transported the world's largest piece of cheese, from
Wisconsin, of course, to the 1964–65 New York World's Fair.
The rig has glass sides because now it displays the world's
largest cheese *replica*, a polystyrene version of the original
14½-by-6½-by-5½-foot cheddar. Now picture 16,000 cows in single file, stretching down the road for 20 miles. *That's* the size
of the herd that gave the milk that made the cheese that went
to the fair.

Chatty Belle, Bullet, and the cheesemobile face Highway 10
on the east edge of town, next to the Wisconsin pavilion—
which, as Chatty Belle explains, represented the state at the
World's Fair. It looks like a party hat with an antenna on top.

W O O D   T I C K   C A P I T A L   O F   T H E   W O R L D
O x b o

*E*ach spring hundreds of people join the ten residents of
Oxbo for the annual wood tick race, a strange little insect
derby that began in 1979. The race takes place in a tent next to
the Oxbo Resort, your basic knotty pine tavern with a couple of
heads on the wall and a few cans of Dinty Moore and Sterno on
the shelf.

Two contestants at a time take their ticks to the racing table
and release them from their little tick carriers (aspirin tins,
film canisters, lockets) onto the center of a bull's-eye target.
The ticks wander around, and the first tick out of the bull's-eye
is the winner of the heat. The mayor of Oxbo smashes the los-
ing tick with a gavel, to ensure that losing-tick genes are not
bred again.

The competition continues until only two ticks remain. The one that survives the championship heat wins a cash prize, a trophy, and a place in the Wood Tick Hall of Fame.

"We have a lot of fun doing something incredibly stupid," says one of the regulars.

The event is held on a Saturday in May. Located just off Highway 70 at the Flambeau River, 15 miles west of Park Falls. Call (715) 762–4786 for details.

WISCONSIN CONCRETE PARK
Phillips

Of all the Wisconsin folks who toted bags of cement for their art, Fred Smith was one of the most prolific. In this Northwoods town he created more than 200 huge figures of animals and people: moose, fish, lions, owls, pioneers, soldiers, angels, kings, and queens. For features and other details he used insulator knobs and pieces of brown beer bottles and bleach bottles and blue Mason jars.

Fred's figures don't just stand there like statues. They're drinking beer, celebrating a double wedding, riding around on horses. The output is amazing for one person, especially considering that Fred didn't get started until age sixty-three. People thought Fred had really gone round the bend when, in about 1950, this fantastical world began to appear in the pine grove next to his Rock Garden Tavern.

Cutting to the chase of the creative urge, Fred confessed, "Nobody knows why I made them. Not even me. The work just came to me naturally."

Fred's place was always a lively gathering spot. The dances and musical events that took place in his barn were legendary,

*Fred Smith remembered friends, local
history, and folklore at his Concrete Park in Phillips.*

with Fred playing fiddle or mandolin and keeping time with
bells strapped to his legs. These days the Friends of Fred Smith
hold an annual celebration in August, with puppets or people
dressed up like the statues acting out the story of Fred's life.

Concrete Park, open year-round, is located on the southern
edge of Phillips on Highway 13. No admission charge, but, as
Fred used to say, "Donations appreciated." Call (800) 269–4505
for more information.

Urban and Rural Wisconsin Legends

1. *Cows—how much should you tip? Cow tipping (the pushing over of a sleeping cow by bored adolescent farm youth before they get the keys to the pickup) appears to occur, along with flicking your Bic on cows' methane emissions and putting the odd goose egg under the odd hen. The domino effect—collapsing an entire chorus line of cows—has never been documented. Two good-size youths working in concert can provide a Holstein with a thrill she'll never forget. One tip: Make sure you push from the uphill side.*

2. *The Cow with the Porthole. Since we're on the subject, yes, there is a cow with a porthole (several in fact) in the dairy barns at the University of Wisconsin in Madison. The device allows access to the fascinating rumens of the ruminates, which gives animal husbanders something to think about (if cows had as many brains as stomachs, they'd be Einsteins instead of Holsteins). Having actually seen a cow with the window of opportunity, I will tell you that I was somewhat disappointed; it was not like the access on a front-loading dryer, and you couldn't see anything going around inside. By the by, the university is working on genetic designer milks by milking white mice. How do they do it? Tiny little stools.*

3. *Sasquatch summers in Wisconsin. A large (if you consider 7 feet tall large), hairy, manlike creature has been sighted numerous times in northern Wisconsin, although most times it turns out to be a*

*large, hairy man. But not always. In 1992 an over-
size hirsute primate with a skunklike odor was
spotted alongside a Jefferson County highway,
standing over a road-killed raccoon, apparently
deciding how to prepare it. The sighting, however,
was by two guys from Illinois who simply may not
be used to folks up here. (Frankly, we've seen worse
in Chicago, and with pinky rings.)*

4. *There are Socialists in the sewers of Milwaukee.
Wrong. The Socialists built the sewers of Milwau-
kee, one of their most fundamental contributions.
Milwaukee had many Socialist politicians and
mayors, until we discovered they were National
Socialists.*

5. *The Virgin Mary has appeared in a bathtub in
Kenosha. True—in fact, in many bathtubs, the
backyard bathtub grotto being endemic to Kenosha*

*and Racine Counties, where religious and handy
Sicilian immigrants, putting in showers during
bathroom remodels, stuck the old tubs on end in
the backyard with the Virgin standing in them.
Some of them are quite elaborate, with masonry,
lights, and, yes, running water. Head out Highway
50 and peek into a lot of backyards.*

6. *An intact flying saucer landed and until recently
was preserved in Appleton, Wisconsin. A case of
mistaken identity—that round, futuristic structure with the rotating lights was actually the Aid
Association for Lutherans, the place for all your
Lutheran insurance needs. Wisconsin has had its
share of sightings, abductions, and ignition points
on squad cars ruined by interference from alien
craft, although most are thought to be from Highland Park, Illinois. Elmwood considered building a
landing strip and beacon for extraterrestrial craft,
so there you go.*

7. *Are those llama herds? Yes, around Eau Claire.
They're ornery beasts, though, and would just as
soon spit as look at you.*

8. *Official NFL gear in Green Bay includes green-and-
gold caskets. Well, maybe not official, but true. Fred
Angermann of Wisconsin Vault and Casket designed
and makes the caskets, which, not being officially
sanctioned by the Packers, do not bear the logo,
although the overall effect is unmistakable. More
than sixty have been sold so far, several have been
interred, and others turn up at tailgate parties at
Lambeau Field. It seems only fitting, since your
only hope at season tickets is in the next lifetime.*

9. *Wisconsin emits strange radio frequencies. It's true. And a lot of it has to do with the Navy. In fact, the claim for the first radio broadcast of any kind is held by a Navy project. In 1917 station 9XM in Madison broadcast exotic AM waves to ships at sea and held on to become the nation's first public radio station, WHA (by chance, the home of Michael Feldman's Whad'Ya Know?).*

Not content with this early success, in the 1980s the Navy constructed a huge and controversial low-frequency antenna that is buried in a giant oval beneath thousands of acres of northern Wisconsin woods. Known alternately as "Project ELF" (for "extremely low frequency") or "Sanguine," it is designed to communicate with submerged nuclear submarines during time of war should everything topside be, shall we say, inoperative. In the event of a third and final world war, the signal to launch will come from us.

10. *Without Wisconsin, there would be no rock 'n' roll. Well, without Wisconsin's Les Paul, there would be no rock 'n' roll as we know it. Working in his garage in West Allis in 1941, Paul attached a string to a railroad tie and came up with the prototype for the solid-body electric guitar, without which Jimmy Page, Pete Townshend, Frank Zappa, and Chuck Berry would not have been possible. Les Paul's first working model was, in fact, dubbed "the log," and later metamorphosed into the beautiful Les Paul Gibson. The solid-body electric guitar allowed sustain and distortion, and if you have sustain and distortion, you have rock 'n' roll.*

Elvis Aron Presley owns and operates historic Bloom's Tavern in Phillips. "Everyone called me Elvis," says the professional Elvis impersonator, "so I decided to legally change my name." And he did. Bloom's is located at 396 South Avon Avenue, just a block off Main Street. The late-nineteenth-century tavern is on the National Register of Historic Places. A sign on the building next door says HEARTBREAK HOTEL—NO VACANCY. *Presley was elected to the Phillips Common Council in 2001.*

FROM YOUNG SHAVERS
MIGHTY CARVERS GROW
Shell Lake

Joseph Barta (1904–72) was a high school math teacher and basketball coach who, for some reason that he could not explain, had wanted to carve the Last Supper since he was sixteen. He'd started carving—"whittling," his family called it—when he was ten.

His family wasn't especially encouraging, either. "You'll cut yourself, Joe," his mother warned. "I'm tired of cleaning up your mess of shavings," his sister complained. Joe wasn't even a churchgoer. Yet the compulsion to carve the monumental piece became almost consuming.

By the time Barta was in his forties, he had left teaching to carve full-time. The Museum of Woodcarving in Shell Lake shows what can happen when you do that. The collection includes hundreds of miniatures (prehistoric creatures; every variety

Joe Barta's Judas.

of cow, dog, and woodland creature; JFK on a campaign swing
through Spooner), and life-size re-creations of biblical figures—
not only the 26-foot-long Last Supper (representing four years
of carving), but Christ from nativity to crucifixion, as well as
Daniel in the lions' den. One of the lions looks like Joseph
Stalin; elsewhere, Herod, from the New Testament, looks like
Adolf Eichmann. A coincidence?

The Barta wood carving collection—the largest created by
one man—was exhibited at the Disney Epcot Center for two
years, but now it is back in northern Wisconsin, where it grew.
The collection is on Highway 63 just north of Shell Lake. Open
daily 9:00 A.M. to 6:00 P.M. from May 1 through October 31.
Call (715) 468–7100 for more details.

WHERE GUYS KEEP SCRATCHING "JFK" ABOVE THE URINAL
Spooner

The Buckhorn Bar on the main street of Spooner is fes-
tooned with taxidermy, as are many taverns in the area.
But particularly noteworthy here are the two-headed calf and
the plaques on the door of the men's room: JOHN F. KENNEDY
USED THESE FACILITIES ON MARCH 18, 1960 and GOVERNOR TOMMY G.
THOMPSON USED THESE FACILITIES ON MAY 3, 1997.

Senator Kennedy had stopped in to shake hands after a
campaign speech outside on the main street of Spooner. He
didn't finish the beer someone bought him, but he did use the
men's room before returning to the campaign trail. It is not
known whether he washed his hands afterward, since he was
not an employee.

Grasping the historic significance of these acts under the
roof of the Buckhorn that day, the owner enshrined the beer

glass in a special case and ordered a plaque for the door. He checked the men's room as well, but saw nothing of museum quality. Thirty-seven years rolled by, and, don't you know, Wisconsin Governor Tommy Thompson drops in one day with some fishing buddies, empties a beer glass, and visits the men's room. And—his secretary was named Kennedy. The plaque in his honor appeared not long afterward.

The Buckhorn is on the corner at 105 Walnut, a block east of Highway 53 on the main business street of Spooner. It also has a beautiful wood-and-glass backbar that the Leinenkugel Brewery installed in the 1930s. For more information call (715) 635–6008.

Manitowish
Waters

45

51 • Sayner

• Minocqua
• Lake Tomahawk

8

45

141

Washington
Island

Gills Rock •
Sister Bay •

Poniatowski
•

Marinette

Oconto •

57

Mosinee •

29 • Embarrass

13

Marshfield

51

Clintonville
• Bear Creek

Rudolph •

Amherst
Junction

Seymour •

Green Bay

Wisconsin
Rapids

Stevens
Point

Black Creek •

• De
Pere

10

45

41

43 • Two Rivers
Manitowoc

Appleton •

13

Neenah •

151

Montello
•

Ripon
•

Oshkosh •

Fond
du Lac •

Kohler • Sheboygan
Sheboygan Falls

Dundee

NORTHEAST

NORTHEAST

The Northwoods, in the upper part of northeast Wisconsin, has a lot of lakes and loons, and its people know how to have a good time. They put costumes on beef roasts and parade them down the street. They wear snowshoes to play baseball.

But the northeast has its serious side. It is the home of world leaders in the manufacture of sauerkraut, toilet seats, and manhole covers. And scattered throughout this part of Wisconsin are champions of all kinds—men who excel at eating bratwurst and Big Macs, champions (at times) of professional football, and a cow named Lucinda who, year after year, gives more milk than any other cow in the world.

As if all this were not enough, at a certain spot in northeast Wisconsin you can stand at the exact center of the northern half of the Western Hemisphere. You'd have to go halfway around the world for another 45' x 90' opportunity like that. Maybe Henry David Thoreau wouldn't have gone "'round the world to count the cats in Zanzibar," but if he'd been near Poniatowski, even he might have sought out this unique geographic spot. So could you.

THINGS THAT GO SLITHER
IN THE NIGHT
Amherst Junction

Conventional wisdom advises against trying to teach a pig to sing because it can't be done and, besides, it annoys the pig.

Worms seem to be another matter. The worms in Amherst Junction can paint pictures and dance, although someone first has to dip them in paint (nontoxic) and play Hawaiian music (the vibrations turn them on). The most accomplished among them is Herman, a 16-inch Canadian earthworm that has not only danced and painted but learned to play basketball.

At the height of his showbiz career, the well-traveled Herman was making the rounds of Hollywood talk shows and doing interviews all over the country. To play basketball he pushed a pea-size basketball across a miniature court and dunked it through a tiny hoop. Painting and dancing came naturally, but teaching Herman to play basketball required quite a large chunk of George Sroda's time.

"I love worms and worms love me," says George Sroda, the Worm Czar of Amherst Junction.

George is Herman's trainer, agent, biographer, and protector from robins. He has a private research laboratory in Amherst Junction where he takes care of millions of earthworms, which he now is more interested in studying than in exposing to the arts. Today he concentrates on their soil and their diet—high in protein, carbs, minerals, and vitamins—and promotes the joys and rewards of raising earthworms. His book *No Angle Left*

Unturned: Facts About Nightcrawlers and Redworms (now in its eighth printing) has inspired thousands of breeders, gardeners, and fishermen to raise earthworms at home as a hobby or a business. Schoolchildren, retirees—anyone with a few dollars and an old refrigerator can do it. To learn more about worms, write to George at Box 97, Amherst Junction, WI 54407, or call (715) 824-3868.

Herman shrank up a bit under the TV lights and retired from showbiz some time ago. *To Tell the Truth, What's My Line,* David Letterman, and Johnny Carson are distant memories. You might say he's living on borrowed time, since the lifespan of a Canadian earthworm is about twenty years, but thanks to George's good care, Herman has not yet gone to that big peat pile in the sky.

HOUDINI: GOT MILK?
Appleton

*B*eing the son of a rabbi, perhaps Harry Houdini's greatest escape was not going to the yeshiva and finding himself a nice little congregation in Appleton. But Harry could wriggle out of rolltop desks, piano cases, coffins, and steamer trunks. Even tossing some such thing into the river—with Houdini in it—was not too much to ask of the greatest escape artist who ever lived.

In one famous trick Houdini told the audience to take a deep breath, took one himself, and then disappeared into a sixty-gallon milk can filled with water. Assistants sealed the can shut. On stage a clock ticked away . . . and away . . . and away. No sign of Houdini. People started to panic and take off, leaving him to reappear to a greatly diminished house.

Sculptor Richard C. Wolter signed the lock on Metamorphosis *"Best wishes, Houdini." It's on a plaza just south of College Avenue, near the intersection with Appleton Street. A marker nearby notes that Houdini was "a high-spirited and troublesome little boy who one night unlocked the front-door locks of all the merchants on College Avenue."*

More of Houdini's amazing deeds are revealed in an interactive exhibit at the Outagamie Museum, along with artifacts related to his life and career.

Houdini spent several idyllic childhood years in Appleton and called it his hometown, although he was born in Hungary. (He died in Detroit of peritonitis, the Tony Curtis movie version of his life notwithstanding.) Houdini's boyhood home and the spot on the Fox River where he nearly drowned are among fifteen locations on a Houdini walking-tour map available at the museum. It explains the presence, elsewhere in Appleton, of the Houdini Lounge, Houdini Elementary School, and Houdini Square.

The Houdini exhibit is at the Outagamie Museum, 330 East College Avenue. The museum also has an Edna Ferber exhibit and walking-tour map. The Ferber and Houdini maps both show where Appleton's favorite daughter interviewed its favorite son for the *Crescent* in 1904. Open year-round 10:00 A.M. to 4:00 P.M. Tuesday through Saturday (and Monday from June through August), noon to 4:00 P.M. Sunday. Admission charge. For more information call (920) 733–8445 or visit www.foxvalleyhistory.org/houdini.

> *reat Lakes Kraut Company of Bear Creek is the world's largest manufacturer of sauerkraut. It produces about 50,000 tons a year (of which four tons is consumed at Lambeau Field by Green Bay Packers fans) and ships much of it to other companies. Its own label is called Krrrisp Kraut.*

THE MEASURE OF A MAN
Black Creek

A few miles south of Black Creek, along Highway 47, are hand lettered signs that shout not about the Apocalypse, not about gun control, but about a humble unit of measurement: the inch.

Some years ago, when he worked as a carpenter, James Franklin Brunette determined that what the United States Bureau of Standards is trying to pass off as the inch is actually 0.9375 of that amount. (Anyone who has ever bought a two-by-four would tend to agree.)

If one barley corn is a third of an inch, and a real inch
measures 0.9375, then . . . um . . .

Beyond Brunette's driveway and scattered throughout his property are many exhibits that demonstrate his intriguing proposition. Wheels and contrivances are covered with millions of numbers, painstakingly hand painted in primary colors to six decimal places, to compare and show the progression of German millimeters, English millimeters, and our joke of a U.S. inch. The most elaborate is his Stonehenge, a huge circle of stones and flags and bags that proves the folly of taking the Bureau of Standards at its word.

Brunette, a.k.a. "Magnifico the Math Master, Arithmetician Extraordinaire," is concerned about the ramifications of it all, for everything from dot-matrix printers to highway safety. He holds forth on the subject at 5107 Highway 47, Black Creek. You can reach him at (920) 739–0733.

IS THAT A GREAT WALL OR WHAT?
Clintonville

Four-wheel-drive technology was developed here early in the twentieth century, and in the 1920s Walter Olen and the Four Wheel Drive Corporation's heavy-duty trucks traveled far and wide. They helped build railways in China, a project that led to Olen's hauling home a hefty souvenir: a portion of the Great Wall of China, which, to date, has protected Clintonville from possible invaders from the north. A gift from revered statesman Sun Yatsen, it is believed to be the only section of the Great Wall ever to leave China.

Eventually Olen's 1,700-year-old Chinese bricks were joined by stones from such places as Jerusalem, the Petrified Forest, Yellowstone National Park, and the Dakota Badlands, along with a Wisconsin millstone. The exotic mementos are lined up in Pioneer Park on the banks of the Pigeon River (where huge

The Great Wall of China at Clintonville.

flocks of pigeons used to roost in the trees) near two historic houses and the Four Wheel Drive Museum, which displays original four-wheel-drive vehicles—a must-visit for SUV or urban assault vehicles seeking to return to their roots. The museum is open from noon to 4:00 P.M. Saturday and Sunday from Memorial Day to Labor Day.

THE LOST DAUPHIN

*I*n De Pere's Lost Dauphin Park there was once a humble log cabin that was thought to have housed the rightful pretender to the throne of France, Prince Louis XVII. He was known in these parts as Eleazer Williams. What distinguished Williams from the average Badger claiming royal descent was the fact that he was a French child who had been placed among the Iroquois Indians of New York at about the time of the Dauphin's death/ disappearance in the Temple in Paris, where his parents and sister were also imprisoned. If the story was to be believed, the sickly dauphin was smuggled out of Paris by his jailer Simon, and with the help of former servants he was transported to the New World and placed among the St. Regis band in New York.

As a missionary and liaison to the Oneida tribe, Williams emigrated with them to Wisconsin in 1821 and became an influential leader—seeking, some said, to establish an Indian kingdom under his rule. His Bourbon origins were apparently unknown to him until a visit made to Green Bay in 1841 by Prince de Joinville, son of King Louis-Philippe. In one of the stranger evenings at the Astor Hotel, the prince informed Williams that he was indeed the son of Louis XVI and Marie Antoinette, offering him a considerable estate if he would renounce all claims to the French throne.

None of us around here was born yesterday, and Williams was no different: He refused to sign and held out for a better deal. Unfortunately, that never came, and he eventually died penniless in his little cabin in the woods.

While the Reverend Williams never assumed the throne of France, it is a fact that for many years following his death, scores of Oneida children were named Eleazer. Visitors can climb the hillside in the park off County Highway D (Lost Dauphin Road), just north of Little Rapids Road, and take in the Fox River—the beautiful domain of the "Lost Dauphin."

THE CHAIR THAT GREW
Embarrass

John Krubsack wanted to grow a chair. This would be harder than growing, say, potatoes or sunflowers. He started out with twenty-eight box elder seeds, drew a chairlike diagram, planted the seeds, watered them, and treated the soil. After about three years—by now it was 1911—the neighbors began to wonder why John was spending so much time nurturing the great tangle of tree growth on his property. Explaining to them that someday they would see a beautiful piece of furniture standing there didn't erase the big question marks over their heads.

As the trees grew, he grafted their trunks together to form legs, back, seat, and arms. For about ten years—chair growing can't be rushed—through wind and snow and sleet, John was there to nurture and protect. Finally it was time to cut all the trees except four—the four legs. The eleventh year he cut the last four, trimmed the trees, put on the final touches, and sighed with satisfaction. His dream of growing a chair had come true. History does not tell us whether he dared to sit down on it.

The chair has been exhibited at museums and fairs around the country and been listed in *Ripley's Believe It or Not*. Today you can see the chair just a block away from where it was originally grown, at Noritage, 220 North Bellevue Street, which manufactures chairs and sofas the usual way, with springs and padding and fabric. The company is owned by the great-grandsons of John Krubsack, who was a banker and a naturalist and not in the furniture business. Its Web site tells more: www.noritage.com.

The chair that John grew.

Embarrass? It was named for its river, whose debris snagged
so many logs that French Canadian lumberjacks called it
Rivière Embarrase (entangle, obstruct).

A Spear and a Beer

Where can you spear a 200-million-year-old living fossil? At Lake Winnebago, in the heart of Wisconsin's Fox Valley. The prize? Hiawatha's Mishe-Nahma, the "King of Fishes," Acipenser fulvescens, a.k.a. the lake sturgeon. They're supposed to be pretty good eating once you pry off the bony plates and smoke 'em. And although the number of females allowed to be

Bill Casper of Fond du Lac at his fishing shack in fair weather. He spearheaded a movement to protect Lake Winnebago sturgeon by founding Sturgeon for Tomorrow.

taken is strictly controlled, it is not impossible to fork some caviar on a very good day.

The catch is that, thanks to much needed conservation limits, the sturgeon season is lightning short, so the window of opportunity closes quickly. You'll need a spear, some beer, a decoy, a chain saw with an ice bar (you may just want to pay the ten bucks and have a hole cut), a permit, and a shanty painted in Packer colors to park on the ice.

If you miss your great white, don't worry—sturgeon can live up to 150 years, which should give you more cracks at catching one than you're probably going to need. The upside is, should the Lord send a sturgeon to your hole, it'll be hard to miss, the record on Winnebago being 6 feet 6 inches and 180 pounds—although that may have been a spearer from last season who just surfaced.

The season opens the second Saturday in February and may close the third, so put down your $10 and take your chances—and don't neglect to be weighed, measured, sexed, and tagged by the waiting DNR biologist, especially if you get a fish. It's not easy—it took one guy from Fond du Lac twenty-three years of drinking Old Style to spear his first sturgeon; hence the saying, "Patience is a sturgeon." If you do get one, they'll hear about it in real time on Jerry Schneider's radio show over WMBE in Chilton.

Oshkosh or Fond du Lac is a good starting point for your sturgeon hunt to Lake Winnebago or one of the smaller lakes, such as Poygan.

THESE WALLS DO TALK
Fond du Lac

If you're worried about what the walls would in fact say could they talk, you might want to get the map of talking houses and historic places from the Fond du Lac Convention and Visitors Bureau to find out which ones to avoid. The map indicates various locations around the city where you can stop the car and tune your radio to a certain number on the dial (not the same one every time) to hear what the house has to say. If you want to have the entire multimedia experience, you can sidle up and peep in the windows. Currently wired are several historic houses—as well as a lighthouse, a bar, a church, and a fire station—although there's nothing to stop you from pulling up to any residence in town and seeing what you can tune in to.

The bar, J. D. Finnegan's on Main Street, was formerly called Schmidt Sample House, and it was the scene of the famous Carrie Nation hatchet-swinging episode on July 18, 1902, when several hefty men had to wrestle a hatchet away from the tenacious Ms. Nation. Today she would probably be swinging away at the sign announcing that Wednesday is ladies night with two drinks for the price of one.

Ms. Nation would, in fact, be beside herself at this decadent downtown intersection of Main and Division. Across the street is a cocktail lounge, in an otherwise respectable hotel that has welcomed such guests as Eleanor Roosevelt, Jack Dempsey, Gene Autry, Wendell Willkie, and John F. Kennedy. On another corner is Dillinger's Dining and Drinking Establishment (Dillinger stopped here for lunch en route to his Northwoods hideout).

Next on the map itinerary, a church tells about a bishop buried inside. Several stops later an impressive nineteenth-century house reminisces about winter days when dozens of neighborhood children gathered in the side yard for skating and tobogganing, and about rainy days when roller skates thundered across the third-floor ballroom.

The tour points out twenty-four historic places, about half of which talk, which may be more than you want to hear from structures of any sort. So, whaddya think—back to Finnegan's?

Free maps are available at the Fond du Lac Convention and Visitors Bureau, 171 South Pioneer Road (east frontage road of Highway 41). The bureau also sells a four-CD Talking Country Roads tour of Fond du Lac County. Call (800) 937–9123 for more information.

A *french fry purchased at Culver's in Wisconsin Rapids in June 2003 was listed as the world's largest french fry on the Internet auction site eBay. It measured 6¾ inches and sold for $202.50.*

WHAT'S GREEN AND GOLD AND LEAPS TALL GRANDSTANDS?
Green Bay

As you approach the Green Bay Packer Hall of Fame in Titletown U.S.A., the landscape grows more green-and-gold. Even the lawn ornaments wear Packer shirts in the famous team colors.

The intense bond between the Packers and their fans became even more apparent when the museum reopened with the recent $295 million renovation of Lambeau Field in 2003. Invited to contribute memorabilia to a room called Titletown's Finest, fans responded in a big way by sending in their treasures. From this embarrassment of riches were selected such items as license plates, a retainer with a Packers *G* made by an orthodontist, a photograph of someone's pet cat in a Packer uniform, and even one of Ray Nitschke's old cigar butts. After months of debate and meditation ("I even prayed about it"), one fan finally parted with a pair of coach Vince Lombardi's shoes.

The shoes ended up in Lombardi's locker in the display that recognizes the twenty Packers in the Pro Football Hall of Fame. Other special exhibits include a re-creation of Lombardi's office (you can even sit at his desk), a slab of concrete from the original tunnel that players used to enter and exit the playing grounds, a diorama of the 1967 Ice Bowl, a padded wall where fans can make their own Lambeau Leap (the touchdown celebration in which the scoring player leaps into the arms of fans in the stands), and, last but not least, the three Super Bowl trophies in a room so ethereal that, says one Packers official, "it's almost like you're in church." Many plaques, artifacts,

*At tailgate parties outside Lambeau Field,
cheeseheads line up to be photographed with Saint Vince
and his guardian angel (John O'Neill and Mary Beth Johnson
of Cross Plains). The money goes to charity.*

videos, and interactive exhibits round out the 25,000-square-foot
museum, the first to celebrate a single professional football team.

The Packers Hall of Fame, 1265 Lombardi Avenue (1⅗ miles
east of Highway 41 from exit 167), is located in the lower level
of the Lambeau Field atrium. Open 9:00 A.M. to 6:00 P.M. daily
year-round except on days of home games when it is open 9:00
A.M. to noon and only to those with tickets to the game.
Admission charge. More at www.packers.com, or call (920)
496–5700.

TAKE THE PLUNGE
Kohler

John Michael Kohler got into the plumbing business in 1883, when he enameled the inside of a dual-purpose horse trough/hog scalder, attached four legs, and sold it to a farmer as a bathtub. Little did he know what he had set in motion.

Today the bathroom products of Kohler Co. are admired near and far. Kohler Co. has artist-edition sinks that are embellished with moss roses and tell fairy tales ("Once upon a time a youth was enamored of a beautiful girl but a frog cast a spell . . ."), or that depict panoramas of Kohler's PGA-worthy Whistling Straits golf course.

A museum at the Kohler Design Center traces the evolution of plumbing fixtures from hog scalder to the Provincial line, with its country meadow of rabbits, birds, and flowers. Original pieces tell the story—zoned bathrooms of the 1940s and 1950s had separate areas for each activity and triggered the master-bedroom suite; gracious-living bathrooms of the 1980s with whirlpool baths and fine furniture introduced sensory appeal.

Across the street free guided "Industry in Action" factory tours walk visitors through the manufacturing process, from the unbaked gray clay to today's ever-popular white, colored, or embellished toilet, sink, or tub. The three-hour tours begin at 8:30 A.M. Monday through Friday. Call (920) 457–3699 to sign up. The Kohler Design Center, 101 Upper Road, is open 9:00 A.M. to 5:00 P.M. Monday through Friday, 10:00 A.M. to 4:00 P.M. Saturday and Sunday. More information can be found at www.kohlerco.com.

You will never look at your toilet the same way again.

The Great Wall of China at Kohler.

FORTY-SIX-INCH SHOES WITH SPIKES
Lake Tomahawk

For people, unlike myself, who've never had the experience of walking around in 46-inch-long shoes, Lake Tomahawk offers a novel form of sport—baseball on snowshoes. Imagine going for a ground ball with contraptions that measure 12 inches wide and nearly 4 feet long attached to your feet! Imagine sliding into second! The 16-inch ball doesn't necessarily make it easier. The action is ludicrous and exciting.

While other slackers have been out curling, the people of Lake Tomahawk have been playing snowshoe baseball for many years and are virtually unbeatable. Sometimes they even play

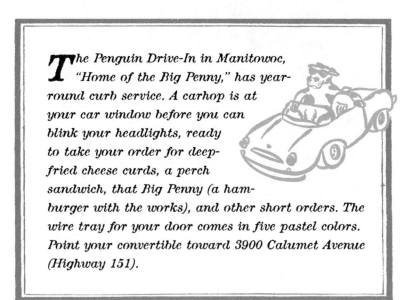

The Penguin Drive-In in Manitowoc, "Home of the Big Penny," has year-round curb service. A carhop is at your car window before you can blink your headlights, ready to take your order for deep-fried cheese curds, a perch sandwich, that Big Penny (a hamburger with the works), and other short orders. The wire tray for your door comes in five pastel colors. Point your convertible toward 3900 Calumet Avenue (Highway 151).

in winter, but it's a shorter, seven-inning game with a blaze-orange ball, given the subzero weather and all that snow. The hope is that someday it will be an Olympic demonstration sport. Wouldn't hurt the Lake Tomahawk economy one bit.

Games are played on Monday nights beginning late in June and ending in mid- to late August (with an extra game on the Fourth of July, before the fireworks). The concession stand opens at 5:00 P.M., and the game starts at 7:30 P.M. Admission is free, and games are held at the Athletic Field, a block west of Highway 47. Call (715) 277-2116.

S H O O T O U T   A T   L I T T L E   B O
M a n i t o w i s h   W a t e r s

If John Dillinger thought things would cool off way up in Manitowish Waters (he is remembered in Fond du Lac, p. 68, and Racine, p.170, for his stopoffs there), he had another think coming. Well-dressed party of ten (John and his boys and their girls) checks in to Little Bohemia Lodge. Hmmm. Isn't April a little early for fishing? Say, wasn't there a lot of excitement up in St. Paul . . . ? Somebody put two and two together and, lo and behold, on the night of April 22, 1934, the FBI showed up. Dogs barked, everybody came out shooting, and Dillinger and the guys got away, though three local men did not because the G-men mistook them for gang members and mowed 'em down. Three months later, on July 22, the Gees took Dillinger down for good outside the Biograph theater in Chicago.

Today the entryway walls of Little Bohemia are papered with newspapers with headlines recalling all the excitement here: "Dillinger Gang Shoots Out of Trap," "Dillinger Abandons Car and Escapes." There's even a love letter from Johnnie to his girlfriend: "Darling: Gee! Honey I am crazy to see you and

when I see you again I am going to take you with me if you
care enough about me to want to go with me . . . lots of love
from Johnnie." The walls of the west wing of the lodge are
riddled with real bullet holes, and a display case shows what
Johnnie and the gang left behind in their hasty departure: the
suitcase they carried the loot in, a can used for target practice,
a suitcase neatly packed with ties and shorts (white with blue
stripes) and shirts, a can of Dr. Lyons tooth powder, two tubes
of Burma-Shave, a box of Ex-Lax. So, Public Enemy Number
One, or just another guy? You be the judge.

All of that was seventy years ago, and today in its big
dining rooms Little Bo (as the regulars having brandy
Manhattans at the bar call the place) serves walleye and ribeye
and roast duck to well-behaved families on vacation. Located on
Highway 51 south of Manitowish Waters. Open mid-April to
mid-January. Lunch served in season from 11:30 A.M., dinner
served from 5:00 P.M. (715) 543–8433.

THE SECRET LIFE OF DENTISTS
Manitowoc

V isitors are flabbergasted when they first enter Rudy Rotter's Museum of Sculpture. His artwork fills an old warehouse that's two stories high and half a block long. Sixteen
thousand pieces!

All this from a dentist who was a late starter as an artist,
and self-taught to boot. Rotter's dental practice was well under
way when he began doing art, creating pieces in his basement
studio in between patients or while waiting for the anesthetic
to take effect. Upstairs he was a perfectionist; downstairs, an
expressionist.

For the pieces on the wall,
self-taught artist Rudy Rotter used teakwood
left over from the multimillion-dollar yachts built by a
former dental patient.

The variety in Rotter's museum is as amazing as the volume: carvings, sculptures, assemblages, drawings. Many of his materials were discards from local industries—aluminum, pattern parts, paper. A box of shiny metal from a junkyard led to lasting ties with Dave's Trophy Company. Rudy transformed everything into art with constant themes: man and woman,

woman and child, family. The Kohler Foundation purchased
200 pieces for its museum collection.

Rudy worked daily in his studio—with soul sister Tosca
singing "Vissi d'Arte" on the CD player—until shortly before he
died in 2001 at the age of eighty-eight.

Rudy Rotter's Museum of Sculpture, 701 Buffalo Street, is
open by appointment only. Call (920) 684–8394. More about
Rudy and his work at www.rudyrotter.com.

JURUSTIC PARK
Marshfield

Long ago, during the Iron Age, creatures inhabited the
McMillan Marsh north of Marshfield. After many centuries
they became extinct. Some succumbed to corrosion from acid
rain. Others were harvested for body parts. Farmers used turtle shells for drinking cups, bird carcasses for shovels, and
legs for bicycle forks . . .

Fortunately, enough body parts survived intact that most
creatures could be reconstructed. We can see them today: the
Whirlysaurus, the largest known airborne marsh creature; the
Bong Bird, whose wing feathers supply the Fiskars plant in
Spencer with blades for grass clippers; the Marsh King, which
dressed in drag and ruled the marsh; the Positron, whose head
bobs in agreement; the Marsh Mouse, which leveled enemies
with methane gas; the Feathered Turtle, slow to get off the
ground but once up, up there for months; Dorks.

These huge and complex rusted-metal creatures and their
history spring from the wide-ranging imagination of Clyde
Wynia, a retired attorney. Where does he get his ideas? "I just

The mighty Marsh Dragon
poses on the grounds of Jurustic Park.

keep digging in the marsh." How long does it take to make
one? He says he doesn't know and doesn't care. "All I want to
do is play."

To get there, turn left off Highway 97 as it leaves Marshfield
onto Highway E. Go about 3½ miles north on E, then west on
U-shaped Sugar Bush Lane ½ mile. More marsh creatures and
malarkey at www.jurustic.com.

DEATH'S DOOR

*I*t's hard to believe that Wisconsin's Nantucket, beautiful Door County, gets its name from Porte des Morts— "Death's Door," the treacherous passage between Green Bay and Lake Michigan that has claimed thousands of vessels and hundreds of lives over the years.

The most famous of these wrecks may have been the explorer La Salle's hide-laden schooner the Griffin, which disappeared in high seas in 1680. The legend of a seemingly impassable strait goes back at least to the ongoing wars between the Winnebago and Potawatomi tribes, which stretched across the passage between the northern tip of the peninsula and Washington Island. A fire beacon set by the Winnebagoes to lead a Potawatomi war party toward the rocky shoals caused a flotilla of canoes to be dashed against the rocks. Hundreds of warriors were killed, and their bodies continued to wash up on nearby Detroit Island for years. In 1871 a hundred vessels were reported lost in "The Door." And in 1913, during the "great blow" when hurricane-force gales lashed the Great Lakes for three November days, twenty ships with 248 men went down. Today, even with sophisticated navigational aids and charts, only the most experienced of sailors attempt the Porte des Morts.

The Door County Maritime Museum in Gills Rock, at 12724 Wisconsin Bay Road, is a good place to learn more about the history of "The Door." And if you would like to sail, boat, or arrange for a charter, the chamber of commerce Web site (www.doorcountyvacations.com) can point you in the right direction.

The Parade of Beef is the creative portion of the annual Beef-A-Rama festival in Minocqua. Local businesspeople cook roasts on their storefront sidewalks, dream up a theme, and then parade the roasts down the main street. Here the Northwoods Wildlife Center, a hospital for injured and orphaned wild animals, tries to revive its entry. The parade ends at Torpy Park, where the roasts are sliced and served up in hundreds of beef sandwiches. Beef-A-Rama usually takes place on the last Saturday in September.

SOME, SEEING A HOLE,
LEAVE IT AT THAT
Montello

Mother Nature gave Montello lakes, rivers, and babbling
brooks. Irving Daggett gave Montello four waterfalls, one
of them 40 feet high, right in the center of town. The waterfall
site was once a working granite quarry, Montello's leading
industry for almost a century. The end of quarrying in 1976

Where once the ground shook at blasting time,
a little musical church plays recorded hymns, and swans glide
across the old granite quarry at Montello.

left Montello with an enormous hole in the ground, but
Daggett, a local realtor and Christmas-tree farmer, saw possibilities there.

He bought the quarry and paid for the construction of the
four falls that tumble year-round into the quarry, which now
is filled with spring water to depths of 100 feet. He also added
a miniature church that rings with religious or patriotic
carillon music at various times throughout the day and, in a
quarry alcove at Christmastime, a life-size nativity scene. The
quarry property occupies about ten acres along Montello
Street (Highway 23) between Daggett Realty and Kwik Trip,
and incorporates a fifth waterfall, which the Lions Club built
back in 1969.

Two other imposing sights lie just west of downtown on
Highway 23 near the Marquette County Courthouse. One is the
largest tree in Wisconsin, a giant cottonwood. The last time it
was measured, in 1978, it was 138 feet high and 23 feet
around. The other is Le Maison Granit, an awesome, plum-
colored mansion built in 1909 of—yes!—Montello granite!

*Granite from the quarry at
Montello won a gold medal at
the 1893 World's Fair as "100%
harder than any other granite."
Purplish-red in color, it was chosen
from more than 280 other granite
samples in 1897 as the monument
stone for Ulysses S. Grant's tomb.*

KISSINGER: MORE THAN A LADY KILLER

*I*t was Henry Kissinger's lucky day when Meldon Maguire came along. Meldon has a dairy farm near Mosinee and serves on the Board of Supervisors.

Late one night in September 1997, along Highway 153 about 9 miles west of Mosinee, Meldon was heading home from a supervisors' meeting and saw flashing taillights up ahead. He stopped his truck at the scene and put on his red "First Responders" vest. (First Responders respond to emergencies and offer assistance.)

Meldon got out and saw guys in suits standing around a big limousine with the windshield all bashed in. The limo had hit a deer. Everybody was okay, and the suits asked Meldon for a ride to their hotel. Meldon cleared out the wrappers and pop cans ("Hey, I got three kids"), everyone piled into the truck, and off they went.

Someone said, "This is Dr. Henry Kissinger," but the name didn't ring a bell. "I knew he had something to do with Nixon," said Meldon, "but I was only about five at that time. I almost asked him what he did for a living. Thank God I didn't."

The next day Meldon received a special invitation to join Kissinger and his entourage, as well as former President Gerald Ford, at the renowned Marshfield Clinic, where an addition was being dedicated to another local boy, Melvin Laird, U.S. secretary of defense in the Nixon cabinet (1969–73).

It was a very full week for Meldon Maguire. He and his wife, Karen, had had a new baby just four days earlier and named her Fawne—before the Kissinger limo–deer accident.

IN MADISON WE CALL THEM PERSONHOLE COVERS
Neenah

No matter how far Badgers may roam, home won't seem quite so far away if they remember to pause at the curb or crosswalk. There they can likely gaze down upon the words NEENAH FOUNDRY CO. NEENAH, WIS.

Most drainage grates and manhole covers bear those words because Neenah Foundry has been meeting the stormwater-management needs of the world for the past century—not only

Even as you sleep, Neenah Foundry is serving you.

manhole covers and drainage gates but also catch-basin covers;
gutter inlets; bridge, subway, and building drains; trench covers; valves and gates; and tree grates. If it's man-made and
drains into the earth, Neenah Foundry is there.

The company began making plowshares in 1872 and later
expanded the product line to include barn-door rollers, sleigh
shoes, bean pots, and other cast-iron items. It cast its first manhole covers and sewer grates in 1904. If you're lucky enough,
you can even get a souvenir manhole cover with your name on
it, like the one that today graces the hearth of Casa Feldman.

NURSE RATCHED, YOU'RE FIRED!
Oshkosh

Northern State Hospital for the Insane admitted its first
patient on April 21, 1873. Many improvements have been
made since that day, including a change of name to Winnebago
Mental Health Institute (WMHI). Today this modern psychiatric
facility treats about 300 children and adults of all ages in its
specialized programs.

A museum on the grounds tells about past practices,
patients, and personnel. On the first floor, exhibits display each
of the twenty-six spoons that one patient swallowed, as well as
an impressive variety of items consumed by others—buttons,
leather straps, a bedspring, scissors, checkers, a rubber heel,
a fingernail file, a toothbrush handle, a thermometer, a crochet
hook, tacks, wire, pieces of slate, and coal. A color photograph
that apparently was taken during surgery shows where several
dollars' worth of change ended up. Another exhibit indicates
the ingenuity of restless patients in making "keys for elope-
ment"—escape, that is—and weapons.

Mourning Becomes DuWayne

*I*don't know about you, but there are mornings when I wake
up and would like nothing more than to blast a bird of
peace, particularly if one's been cooing outside my window since
six. Well, in September 2003, after a two-year court battle, Wisconsin's first-ever dove season opened.

It all had begun when 22,000 of the 27,000 or so people who
turned out for a Natural Resources Board meeting (which usually draws as many as 37) voted to shoot the Official State Bird
of Peace.

DuWayne Johnsrud, a state legislator from Eastman, led
the charge against the admittedly not very hard to take dove
(whose mourning, after all, does have a "u" in it). He even went
so far as to fricassee a mess of them in his capitol office (don't
know where he got them, but there were noticeably fewer pigeons
on the porticos that week) and offer tiny little drumsticks to all
takers to make his point. Taste-wise, they are said to run somewhat to the crow side of squab; but as the French say, the sauce
is everything. Johnsrud noted, "There are those people out there
who don't want you to eat anything that's got a face on it."

The season ran from September through October, with a
limit of fifteen things with faces on them per day. It offered a
special challenge to hunters because mourning doves fly errati-
cally, even when they're not being fired upon. The cleverest
mourning doves spent most of those two months perched on
power lines after word spread that a utility company had
warned hunters that all kinds of problems could result from
shooting at birds on power lines. Each bird that did not survive
the season rewarded the hunter with about half an ounce of
mourning dove.

The downside is that at one time, Wisconsin had the largest
nestings of the now extinct passenger pigeon, which in 1871
packed some 850 square miles at one sitting—an estimated 136
million birds. The last was shot by a conservationist in 1899,
making the woods safe, once again, for acorns.

If this sort of thing interests you, you can contact the
Department of Natural Resources regarding mourning
doves, as well as other things with faces that you can hunt
in Wisconsin. Call (608) 266–2621 or visit the Web site at
www.dnr.state.wi.us.

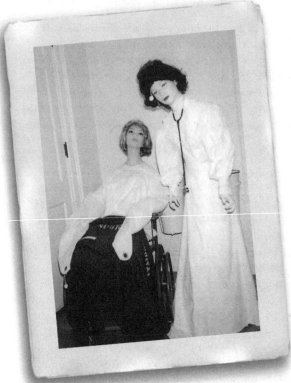

A well-coiffed mannequin models a straitjacket, a relic of the Northern State Hospital for the Insane, now Winnebago Mental Health Institute.

Upstairs are five more rooms of exhibits. They include uniforms that staff members formerly wore (today they usually wear street clothes), an electroshock-therapy machine, medical instruments in cabinets, mannequins in treatment, a wicker body basket, and laboratory equipment. Photographs and an audiocassette offer further details from the past, such as statistics on lobotomies. The entire presentation helps visitors appreciate the progress that has been made over the past century in treating troubled individuals along the shores of Asylum Bay on Lake Winnebago.

The Juliane Farrow Museum, at 4150 Sherman, is housed in what formerly was the superintendent's residence; it includes many original furnishings. The museum is located in the northwest part of the 250-acre grounds that WMHI shares with Wisconsin Resource Center (for about 500 corrections inmates with mental health problems) and the Drug and Alcohol Correctional Center (population about 200). It is located a few miles north of Oshkosh.

From exit 120 eastbound (Highway 110/Algoma Boulevard) of Highway 41, immediately take the first left turn (Snell Road) and follow Snell for about 4 miles. It leads directly to the grounds. The museum is open from 1:00 to 3:30 P.M. on Thursday only, from February through October. For more information call (920) 235–4910, ext. 2345.

LEAPIN' LIZARDS
Oshkosh

If you didn't find just the right statuary for the garden at FAST in Sparta (p. 224), you might browse the grounds of Schettl's near Oshkosh. The main business of Schettl's Freight Sales is hardware and building supplies, but its line of "so-tacky-it's-way-beyond-cool stuff," as one admirer puts it, is the big attraction here. Gigantic insects, roosters, circus animals, sharks, sundaes, and cowboy boots. They cover the ground, they perch on rooftops, they bound through the air. Elephants look striking against the backdrop of barn, silo, and cornfields across the road.

How many dinosaurs do you know that have black leather seats? The one at Schettl's does. Just climb a flight of stairs to mouth level, step right in, and settle down, the better to admire the rest of the decor, which carries out a prehistoric theme—

You Went a Long Way, Baby Doe

*H*er eyes were blue—bluer than Lake Winnebago—her ankles were strong, and her hemline revealed more of her lower extremities (it wasn't nice to say "legs") than the Oshkosh of 1877 was accustomed to seeing. The only female entrant in the figure-skating contest, Elizabeth Bonduel McCourt won first place, the box of chocolates, and the heart of a handsome spectator, Harvey Doe.

The couple married and moved to the mining town of Central City, Colorado, where Harvey proceeded to run his share of the Doe family fortune into a shoestring. The mine shut down, and so did the marriage ("You have of corse herd of my sad sad loss in loosing my darling Babe I am heart broken about it I shal go crazey," sniveled Harvey in a letter home to the folks in Oshkosh). But new possibilities opened up for Elizabeth, or "Baby." (She acquired the nickname in the rowdy mining towns, as in "There goes a beautiful —.")

In time Baby's picture was appearing on saloon beer trays and calendars, and at Leadville she met Horace Tabor, whose silver mines had made him one of the wealthiest men in the West and, by appointment, a United States senator. His plain and plucky wife, Augusta, could not compete.

In 1883 Horace and Baby celebrated their wedding at the Willard Hotel in Washington, D.C. (Baby stopped off in Oshkosh to model her silks and furs for the town gossips). President Chester Arthur, distinguished guests, and a contingent from Oshkosh attended. Baby's gift from Horace was a $75,000 necklace of jewels that Queen Isabella had hocked so that Columbus could discover America. Later they had two daughters, Elizabeth Bonduel Lillie Tabor and Rosemary Echo Silver Dollar Honeymoon Tabor ("Silver Dollar" for short).

Does Oshkosh have a statue, a plaza, or even a bench at the skating rink in memory of the "Silver Queen," the most fabulous woman to emerge from its pioneer era—this Marla Maples, this Monica of the Middle West? It does not, and the Colorado Historical Society has all of Baby Doe's memorabilia, leaving not so much as a maribou feather from her $7,000 wedding gown for the folks back in Wisconsin. But in 1972 the University of Wisconsin–Oshkosh produced The Ballad of Baby Doe, the 1956 opera by Douglas Moore that had its New York City Opera premiere in 1958 and by now is recognized as the quintessential American opera. It's got politics! the Wild West!! the American dream!!!

The Ballad of Baby Doe tells the whole story, right down to the day in 1935 that Baby Doe was found dead—frozen with two weeks' stiffness into the shape of a cross—in a shack outside Horace's Matchless Mine. Horace had gone bankrupt years earlier when the country abandoned the silver standard. "Hang on to the Matchless. It will make millions again," were his dying words in 1899. And that is what Baby Doe did, though it meant shuffling around town with gunnysacks on her feet for shoes in her last years, and finally dying in rags.

A safari at Schettl's ends badly when a rhino tips over a
Suzuki with Texas plates and a headless driver.

the little nest of baby dinosaurs, the dragon collection on the windowsill.

This would also be the place to shop for Cinderella's coach. Schettl's has several and shows them bearing such passengers as a mountain goat, an Egyptian mummy, and a blonde vamp in a red, white, and blue miniskirt. Other outsize display cases resemble glass gazebos and are occupied by British royalty, Laurel and Hardy, Marilyn Monroe, and Elvis. Display is definitely Mel Schettl's forte.

After you remember what you came to Shettl's for—
bathtubs? siding? batteries?—you can consider taking home
something special that may have caught your eye. A life-size
set of Blues Brothers, the moose that ate Oshkosh, the Statue
of Liberty. The vast collection is available for rent, and some of
it is for sale.

Schettl's is at 5105 Highway 110, which is parallel to
Highway 41, and a few miles north of Oshkosh. Hours are
8:00 A.M. to 8:00 P.M. during the week, 8:00 A.M. to 5:00 P.M.
Saturday, and 11:00 A.M. to 4:00 P.M. Sunday. More at
www.mschettl.com.

Bemis Manufacturing Company
of Sheboygan Falls is the
world's largest manufacturer of
toilet seats.

A MAN. A PLAN, PONIATOWSKI
Poniatowski

About 5,000 people from all over the world have driven a
maze of county roads in search of a certain 1885 white
frame building with a Blatz sign out front.

It was Gesicki's Bar, the home of the 45 x 90 Club, and
behind the bar was the membership book that everyone came to

sign. It attested that they had stood in the exact center of the northern half of the western hemisphere—45 degrees north latitude and 90 degrees west longitude, or halfway between the North Pole and the equator, and halfway between the Greenwich meridian and the International Date Line. Of the other three spots like it on the globe, two are under water; the third is in the middle of China.

John Gesicki instigated the official recognition and landmark. He had a little park outside of town all ready when the U.S. Geological Survey came to plant the marker in 1969. He started the club. After John died, his widow, Loretta, offered the book and the pen. But the membership book is closed now. In 2003 Loretta decided she needed a rest, so she sold the bar, packed up the book, and moved to an apartment in Wausau. What once was Gesicki's Bar is now a private residence.

When Poniatowski pilgrims came in the door, Loretta used to play a recording of Peter and Lou Berryman singing this song:

Exactly half the way from the Equator to the Pole
A quarter of the way around the planet as a whole
It's very hard to find it on a map o' county roads
Ridiculously easy on a four-inch globe

Magellan's men said Captain have we gotten very far
We're writing to our mothers just to tell 'em where we are
The Captain said our longitude is fifty on the dot
I don't know where we are but I can tell you where we're not.

A quarter of the way from top to bottom of our earth
A quarter of the way around the planet of our birth
Speaking cartographically it's not extreme to say
It's the most important 'towski in the USA.

What is on the tip of every schoolkid's tongue
What I mean of course besides a wad of gum
The name of a location every grownup knows
Of a church, a couple taverns, and a school that's closed.

I asked an old cartographer where he would rather be
He mumbled there's a place that's always fascinated me
I'll prob'ly mispronounce it he admitted with a sigh
It's P-O-N-I-A-T-O "duBULLYU" s-k-i.
Poniatowski . . .

Poniatowski is located about 12 miles west of Wausau and
does not appear on all maps. From Highway 29 west of
Wausau, go north on Highway H, then west on Highway U to
Poniatowski. Follow the signs to the spot that marks the center
of the northern half of the Western Hemisphere.

ODD BEDFELLOWS
Ripon

R ipon has the distinction of being the birthplace of both the
Republican Party and the Wisconsin Phalanx, a distinctly
Badger take on Communism in which stock was sold, real
estate purchased, and communal adherents rewarded according to their usefulness.

The Socialist band was organized in Kenosha and led in the
spring of 1844 to the Ceresco Valley (named for Ceres, the god-
dess of grain) near Ripon by Warren Chase, a follower of
Fourier. The group planted grain and built a gristmill, carpenter shop, school, and the longhouse (which still stands today).
Although it was ideal, it was not free. Board was 63 cents a
week (on the other hand, wages averaged out to 7½ cents an
hour, and the cost of feeding and clothing the entire extended
family was deducted). And while it promoted equality, some
were more equal than others in their skills—which, in time,
caused some resentment by the less useful.

Still, Utopia does not mean "nowhere" for nothing. Ceresco was a success until a life without "rum, vulgarity, and profanity" seemed to wear on some, particularly after free-love devotees moved in. Others, tired of communal life, set up their own households. But at its height, 200 Communists lived in rural Ripon, some of whom, idealists still, stayed on after the community was sold off in 1850 to join in the formation of the Republican Party, the flower of the strong Wisconsin antislavery movement.

The one-room schoolhouse where this meeting took place on March 20, 1854, is now a historic site at 303 Blackburn Street, about a block off Ripon's main street. The longhouse is at 26–34 Warren Street.

PRAISE THE LORD AND PASS THE MORTAR
Rudolph

The Grotto Gardens and Wonder Cave represent the lifelong labors of parish priest Phillip J. Wagner. This site is all the more remarkable if you know that Wagner started here with a potato field and no mortaring experience. His first attempt at grotto building, in 1928, consisted of stacking up rocks. When he realized he'd also need mortar, he stirred it in a bread pan with a kitchen spoon. He got the hang of it, though, and over the next thirty years, Wagner and an equally dedicated member of the parish transformed the potato field into an extraordinary collection of shrines and grottoes.

The Wonder Cave makes this religious grotto unique among others in Wisconsin. From the outside the Wonder Cave looks like a hill of rocks among trees and plantings. Inside, however, it has not only cave ambience—a passageway that winds up and down and around, water trickling down the walls—but also organ music, statuary, and biblical reminders in the form of little tin sheets with perforated words and images, back-lighted with colored bulbs. The cave is entirely above ground (unusual for a cave), and the man-made passageway is a fifth of a mile long.

The Grotto Gardens and Wonder Cave at Rudolph are located on the grounds of St. Philip's Parish, 6957 Grotto Avenue. The Wonder Cave and a gift shop are open daily 10:00 A.M. to 5:00 P.M. Memorial Day through Labor Day. The Grotto Gardens are open year-round, no charge; there's a small admission fee for the Wonder Cave. For more information call (715) 435-3120.

THE WOODS ARE ALIVE WITH THE SOUND OF MOTOR TOBOGGANS
Sayner

*E*ighty years ago Carl Eliason rigged up the world's first snowmobile by combining an outboard motor, part of a Ford Model T radiator, two bicycle chains, and two pairs of downhill skis. He painted the seat red and called the whole thing a motor toboggan. In the garage behind Eliason's Grocery, he kept on fiddling with the design and built forty more motor toboggans, almost no two alike. For quite a few years Eliason Snowmobile Manufacture had the field to itself, but then along came the competition and their copywriters, with names such as Arctic Cat, Ski-Doo, Sno-Traveler, and the Ice Cycle (a 1964 creation that was supposed to be portable but turned out to be too heavy to lug from the family station wagon to the ice). These share a room but not center stage with Eliason's motor toboggan at the Vilas County Historical Museum. Some rare outboard motors are here, too, as well as a hand-powered motor made of wood, carved propellor and all.

The museum has much, much more. Beyond the armies of old dolls and passels of sewing machines and typewriters and kitchen equipment is a room of surprises in taxidermy: wildebeest, cape Buffalo, warthog, eland—all strangers to this neck of the woods. They're the trophies of a Sayner man who had had his fill of white-tailed deer and went after big game in Africa.

Look for the lumberjack with the big blue ox outside 217 Main Street (Highway 155) in Sayner, just 1 block north of Highway N. Open 10:00 A.M. to 4:00 P.M. daily from Memorial Day to mid-October. Call (715) 542–3388 for more information, or visit www.northern-wisconsin.com/museum.

ELEGY FOR A SPATULA
Seymour

Charlie Nagreen of Hortonville was only fifteen years old in 1885 when he arrived in Seymour by ox-drawn wagon to set up his meatball stand at the Outagamie County Fair. When meatballs turned out to be not the ideal finger food (especially since he cooked them in butter), Charlie smooshed the meatball between two slices of bread and called it a hamburger.

For the next sixty-five years, Hamburger Charlie was a fixture at the fair. In 1989 Seymour underlined its place in culinary history by cooking and serving to 13,000 people a 5,520-pound hamburger—the world's largest, as recorded in the *Guinness Book of World Records*. When you come to think of it, it's amazing they had to go that high to get the record.

In 1999 word arrived from Montana of a 6,040-pound hamburger. Home of the Hamburger, Inc., graciously hung

*The grill that cooked the
world's biggest burger. They didn't try to flip it.*

back until 2001 to let the Montanans bask in glory, and then
cooked an 8,266-pound burger (about fifty-three cows' worth)
to reclaim the title.

The Hamburger Hall of Fame museum on Main Street,
which documented Seymour's place in hamburger history, is no
longer open, and whether Charlie's spatula will find a new
home is in question. But the annual Burger Fest, with parade,
bun run, bun toss, and ketchup slide, remains an annual event,
the first Saturday in August.

A cure for cabin fever in 1939,

smelt wrestling at the Smelt Carnival in Marinette.

FROM PLUMBING, ART

Sheboygan

When visitors enter the washrooms at the John Michael Kohler Arts Center, they usually stay inside for a long time. There's a lot to see.

One of the men's rooms tells the social history of architecture in vivid hand-painted tiles, with such phrases posted over the fixtures as "Celebrating Another Conquest," "Boldness Has Genius," "Aspiring Toward Heaven," and "Defending the Castle." Behind tinted-glass cartouches in a women's room are etched the thoughts of Isadora Duncan, Frida Kahlo, and eight other women. Squeezing a bulb attached to each creates a shower of cosmetic powders and soap shavings behind the glass.

The six artist-decorated washrooms are one result of the unique Arts/Industry residency program funded by Kohler Co., which encourages artists to explore materials and equipment at its plumbingware factory. The collaboration has produced many more works, some of which appear in one of the galleries. They include a large coffee cup that flushes, Ken and Barbie andirons, and a Squeaky Fromme nightlight.

Another gallery exhibits works of self-taught Midwestern artists. Among them have been the elaborate chicken- and turkey-bone towers of the prolific artist Eugene Von Bruenchenhein, a Milwaukee baker who so adored his wife, Marie, that he fashioned elegant crowns of ordinary materials for her. Another time it invited Sheboyganians to create art measuring no more than 1-inch-by-1-inch-by-1-inch and displayed their 1,700 pieces—tiny paintings and sculptures and furniture— along measuring tapes.

There are surprises elsewhere, too, such as the life-size ceramic horse by Deborah Butterfield in the formal dining room of the Kohler family mansion, which stands at the corner of the recently expanded Arts Center.

This water-pistol bouquet in delft style, with hand-painted and hand-glazed tiles, appears over a urinal at the Kohler Arts Center. The artist was Ann Agee.

The John Michael Kohler Arts Center, 608 New York Avenue, opens at 10:00 A.M. daily, year-round. (Be there when the doors open and you probably can safely tour all six washrooms. At other times try a stakeout, followed by a knock on the door.) It closes at 5:00 P.M. Monday, Wednesday, and Friday; at 8:00 P.M. Tuesday and Thursday; and at 4:00 P.M. Saturday and Sunday.

To get here take exit I–43 (exit 126) onto Highway 23 East, which becomes Kohler Memorial Drive and then Erie Avenue. Continue east to Sixth Street, turn right, and follow Sixth Street 4 blocks south to New York Avenue. The entrance to the Arts Center is on New York Avenue between Sixth and Seventh Streets. Call (920) 458–6144 for more information, or visit www.jmkac.org.

THE WRECK OF THE LOTTIE COOPER
Sheboygan

T he *Lottie Cooper* was a three-masted schooner that foundered in a howling northeast gale on the night of April 9, 1894. It went down in the Sheboygan harbor and lay there for the next century. Recently her remains were discovered on the harbor floor, during surveying work for construction of a marina. The remains were recovered from the murky floor, reassembled in their original positions, and are now on display on the grounds of the marina.

Divers report greatly improved visibility
when a shipwreck, like the Lottie Cooper *in Sheboygan, is on land.*

An estimated 10,000 ships have been lost on the Great Lakes—700 in Lake Michigan, 60 off Sheboygan, and about a dozen right in the harbor. (Some were hauled up, pumped out, and put back in service, only to sink two or three more times.) *Lottie* represents them all because she's the only recovered shipwreck on display on the Great Lakes today. Text and drawings tell more about her saga.

There are self-tours here as well as guided tours for groups. Call (920) 458–2974 for information.

SHEBOYGAN SAYS "ALOHA!"
Sheboygan

From bratwurst to surfing, Sheboygan constantly surprises. The annual Dairyland Surf Classic held at Northside Beach is the largest freshwater surfing competition in the world, and its champion is Larry Williams, who surfs here almost year-round.

The water is pretty cold in August—what must January be like? Mostly frozen, says Larry (a.k.a. Longboard), who leashes his ankle to his board so it doesn't get away "because it's quite a challenge to retrieve a board that's trapped under an iceberg." An iceberg? Yes, icebergs, snow squalls, legendary gales, and waves larger than 24 feet several times a year. Having surfed here for more than thirty years, he knows his Lake Michigan.

Mercifully, the Dairyland Classic takes place in summer, over Labor Day weekend, and it attracts surfers from as far away as Australia, Hawaii, and New Zealand. You can see Larry and his twin brother, Lee (a.k.a. the Water Flea), in *Step into Liquid* (a kind of *Endless Summer, Part 3*), which was filmed here and elsewhere in 2000 and won Best Documentary at the 2003 Maui Film Festival.

AND SWEDISH MEATBALLS
UNDER THE ROOF
Sister Bay

R egardless of whether or not Scandinavian houses still have sod roofs, Al Johnson thought a sod roof would be a nice touch for the Swedish restaurant he opened in 1948. The eatery was housed in a log building that was shipped in pieces from Norway to Sister Bay. A friend donated a goat named Oscar to complete the picture, and after that Al didn't have to worry about advertising. The word spread, crowds gathered, and they still do.

Al Johnson's goats.

It's best to arrive in some conventional manner, such as by
car or on foot. When curious people from Marinette landed
their helicopter on the lawn just north of the restaurant one
day, the terrified goat leaped off the roof, hurdled a parked car,
dodged through traffic, jumped into the bay, and started
swimming. Al had to chase after it in a boat for the rescue.

Today six or eight goats munch away up there, while diners
below select from a more interesting menu, starting with
Swedish pancakes with lingonberries for breakfast. Al Johnson's Swedish Restaurant is open 6:00 A.M. to 9:00 P.M. daily.
It's located on Bayshore Drive (Highway 42). Call (920)
854–2626 for information.

THAT'S USING YOUR CHEESE

*In November 1995 Frank Emmert Jr., a die-
hard Green Bay Packer fan, was flying home
to Superior from a Packers-Browns game in
Cleveland. As he neared Stevens Point, ice
caused his single-engine plane to lose power.
Just before impact Emmert grabbed the foam-
rubber cheesehead he'd worn at the game and
buried his face in it. He believes it saved his face
and arms from serious injury (though not his
ankle), and maybe even his life.*

*National wire services picked up the story,
and before long Emmert was being wheeled onto
the set of* The Tonight Show *in a cart that
resembled a cheese wedge to tell the story to Jay
Leno. Today he still travels with his cheesehead.*

TONY'S FAN FAIR
Stevens Point

One day in the 1940s, while Anton Flatoff was working at the Whiting Hotel downtown, he saw an old exhaust fan in the trash. Whoever was remodeling the hotel kitchen didn't have Tony's imagination. He took it home; this was the first of many exhaust fans to catch his eye over the years.

Tony's Fan Fair started with
an old exhaust fan from the hotel downtown.

Tony eventually painted the fans red, white, and blue, added some wheels and cool industrial shapes, and assembled "Tony's Fan Fair" in his backyard. It's about 15 feet tall, and when the wind blows, the fans spin and make a soft rattley sound.

On the west edge of Stevens Point, after the intersection of westbound Highway 10 and County Highway C, look to the right from Highway 10 toward the first house on Harding Avenue. Or pull up at 556 West Harding for a closer look. Even the shutters on Tony's house are decorated with little fan blades.

LITTLE ICELAND

*W*ashington Island is the oldest Icelandic community in the United States, which is one reason that old iconoclast Thorstein Veblen spent summers there from 1908 to 1926, studying and writing and brushing up on his Icelandic. He'd got **The Theory of the Leisure Class** out of his system by that time, but more writing along those lines followed in the secluded cabin he built for himself. Every morning he rowed across Little Lake to chitchat in Icelandic with the Bjarnarssons and pick up fresh milk and butter.

POSSIBLY A COW
JUMPING OVER THE MOON?

Most alien craft streaking through Wisconsin are shiny, lighted, wedge-shaped BMWs from Chicago's North Shore, hurtling their crews toward their holiday cabins, but our state is no stranger to craft from somewhere far, far beyond Illinois. In fact, one of the first recorded UFO sightings in America was reported in Eagle on April 14, 1897. A craft "looking like a toy balloon" with red and blue lights hovered near the northern horizon—much amazing Otto Lantz, Dr. Colter, and Will Raiche—before flying on to perplex other communities, including Oconto, Marinette, Darlington, Marshfield, Eau Claire, Kenosha, Madison, Rio, Ripon, and Baraboo (where some skeptics thought it may have had a home base in the Ringling Brothers cosmos).

Dundee Mountain, near the town of Osceola, is a favorite gathering place for those who have seen long, glowing, cigar-shaped or red, triangular hovering objects. They come here hoping for another glimpse—or, in some cases, another proctological examination. Bob Kuehn of Fond du Lac, who attends every year, has seen sixty-five UFOs over the years, the first being a flying washtub when he was four. Bill Benson, the owner of Benson's Hide-A-Way on Long Lake at Dundee and the man behind UFO Daze, an annual summertime event, believes there have been so many sightings in what he considers Wisconsin's Area 51 (of Roswell, New Mexico, fame) because of either our latitude or longitude. Or perhaps it's for the same reason that the beer makers came: "We also have a lot of good water here." Sightings have occurred regularly in Long Lake since an alien craft followed a farmer plowing in 1948.

Jay Rath, in his book The W-Files, cites a Vilas County report of local Joe Simonton's close encounter with a flying saucer "brighter than chrome." It landed in his backyard, disgorging three aliens who served him pancakes that "tasted like cardboard" (which many believe had to be Norwegians bearing lefse). Rath lists several hundred other reported sightings around the state—which, in toto, have got to add up to more than just cabin fever. Belleville and Elmwood (you know, where they planned the UFO landing strip?) both have UFO days, and Bill Benson can fill you in on the latest around Long Lake. The number to call is (920) 533–8219.

TOOTIE LOVES CHUCK
Two Rivers

Two Rivers is the birthplace of both the ice-cream sundae and Charlton Heston's wife. A re-creation of the soda fountain where Edward Berner first poured chocolate sauce over ice cream in 1881 is among the exhibits at the old Washington House hotel. Less well known but popular for many years, according to a news story posted here, was a 5-cent float consisting of a tall glass of milk, a scoop of ice cream, and crushed oyster crackers.

In the Sons and Daughters Room is an exhibit devoted to Lydia Clarke Heston, who is not only the wife of movie actor Heston but also the great-great-granddaughter of Hezekiah Huntington Smith, a founder of Two Rivers. Lydia is pictured in her own acting days and with other swimmers in the Polliwog Club of Washington High School. Her annual Christmas letters to a longtime friend and "all of you back in God's country" are here, too. Signed "Tootie and Chuck," several years' worth of newsy letters, each four or five typewritten pages long, are on display, which include some reminiscences, such as the day in 1944 in Greensboro, North Carolina, when "we went for a stroll amid the blooming spring. We passed a small white church with a flowering cherry tree. We tiptoed inside and an hour later we were Sergeant and Mrs. Charlton Heston." The exhibit also reports Chuck's retirement as president of the National Rifle Association.

The second floor of Washington House is something like a Wisconsin Sistine Chapel. The walls and ceiling are covered with generic pastoral and patriotic scenes that were created by mural artists in 1906 and restored by a conservator in the 1990s. Originally the room was used for dances, plays, and wrestling matches; today it's the site of concerts, lectures, and other community events.

Washington House is 1 block east of the main street in Two Rivers ("T'rivers" as the natives call it) at Seventeenth and Jefferson Streets, across from a large museum of wood type, and down the street from a history museum that used to be a convent. Open daily year-round from 9:00 A.M. to 9:00 P.M. May through October; 9:00 A.M. to 5:00 P.M. November through April. Call (920) 793–2490 for more information.

In Oshkosh in September 2003, four men claimed the world's record for the longest continuous drum roll. Taking turns (ten minutes apiece), they drummed for twelve hours, almost three hours longer than the previous time listed in the Guinness Book of World Records.

NELSEN'S BITTERS CLUB
Washington Island

Bartenders everywhere keep a small bottle of bitters on hand for flavoring drinks—Manhattans usually, and then they use only a dash. But Nelsen's orders bitters by the case, having been a world leader in its consumption ever since the days of Prohibition.

It was then that resourceful Tom Nelsen, who had worked in a bitters factory in Europe before coming to Washington Island, licensed his tavern as a drugstore, upon discovering that bitters was classified as a medicine. (A Prussian surgeon and veteran of the Battle of Waterloo had concocted it for the upset stomachs of Simon Bolivar's freedom fighters in Venezuela.) At 44.7 percent alcohol, the equivalent of 90-proof whiskey, bitters became a popular remedy on the island, although for what is still subject to some debate.

In time the extraordinary consumption of bitters prompted a letter of inquiry from the House of Angostura of Trinidad and Tobago ("By Appointment to Her Majesty") to its very best customer—Nelsen's stocks only the Angostura label—and was surprised to learn that residents of a tiny island were drinking it straight. They still do.

The exact content of Angostura bitters is a deep dark secret, but it's a distillation of various tropical herbs, barks, and roots. Tom Nelsen drank a pint a day and lived to almost ninety, a good enough reason for islanders still to drop in for "a tapper and a shot of bitters."

In the 1950s Tom's nephew Gunnar started the Bitters Club, which is still going strong. Every year thousands of people join the club by tossing down a shot of bitters and signing the book. Nelsen's Hall Bitters Pub and Restaurant, open year-round, is on Main Road, about 1½ miles north of the ferry dock. It celebrated its centennial in 1999, and, by foiling the feds during Prohibition, it is the bar with the longest continuous run in Wisconsin. Call (920) 847–2496 for more information.

A lawn jockey in Packer gear, on Highway 22 just
north of the Columbia County–Marquette County line.

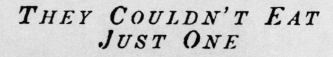

THEY COULDN'T EAT JUST ONE

*I*n the 1860s, a woodcutter named John A. "Long John" Johnson was well known around Sister Bay for his huge appetite. In Exploring Door County, *Craig Charles writes that a local store-keeper bet Long John five dollars that he couldn't eat five dozen eggs in one sitting. A quixotic bet to be sure, but the big guy took it "on the condition the prize included a pint of whiskey. Long John is said to have eaten all the eggs, drunk the whiskey and gone home to top it off with a loaf of bread and a pail of milk."*

More than a century later, Wisconsin men are carrying on this proud tradition. One possible rein-carnation of Long John is Dennis Leffin of Kohler, who as a growing boy in the 1950s won not only more bratwurst-eating contests than anyone in the history of Sheboygan County but also eating con-tests in watermelon, ice cream, and sauerkraut. Not on the same day, we hope.

Don Gorske of Fond du Lac has outdone both men with a style that's more distance than speed. He has eaten one or two Big Macs every day for more than thirty years, and when Wisconsin Curiosi-ties talked with him (in October 2003), he had just finished his 19,433rd Big Mac. He has kept track ever since May 17, 1972, the day a Big Mac first filled his mouth with joy. Actually he had nine of them that day (they cost 49 cents then) and 265 in the first month, as he discovered when he cleaned out—and counted—the Big Mac pods in the back-seat of his car.

Since then he has kept count in little calendar-notebooks (he admits to being a wee bit obsessive), which impressed the Guinness people, who declared him the record holder when he passed the 18,000 mark. (At that point, a math class at a Fond du Lac high school figured out that number of Big Macs represented 14 beef cattle, 560 pounds of cheese, and 100 gallons of Special Sauce.) But Gorske kept on going because he truly loves Big Macs. Nothing else appeals to him, so every day, after work as a prison guard in Waupun, he goes to McDonald's on Military Road in Fond du Lac for a Big Mac or two. He also has had Big Macs in forty-eight states (and received them by mail from the other two, Alaska and Hawaii); at such U.S. landmarks as the Grand Canyon, Niagara Falls, and Alcatraz Island; and at every major league baseball stadium, NFL stadium, and NASCAR track in the country.

Gorske is trim—6 feet 2 inches, 179 pounds—and healthy (cholesterol 140). He read in Newsweek that McDonald's defense attorneys had invoked him at trial in an obesity lawsuit brought by plaintiffs who must have been chasing their Big Macs with 32-ounce triple-thick shakes. Over the years he has missed only eight days of Big Macs, sometimes because of travel (incredibly, no golden arches appeared on the landscape) or blizzards—he'd have been there, but the place was closed.

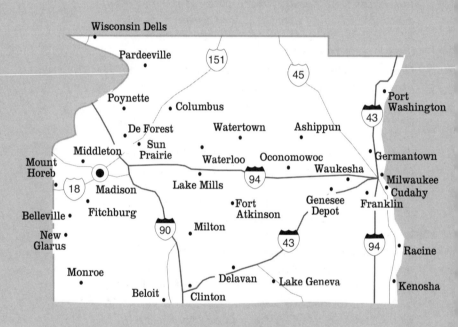

Wisconsin Dells

Pardeeville

151

45

Poynette

Columbus

Port
Washington

43

De Forest

Watertown

Ashippun

Germantown

Middleton

Sun
Prairie

Waterloo

Oconomowoc

Mount
Horeb

Waukesha

Milwaukee

94

18

Madison

Lake Mills

94

Cudahy

Belleville

Fitchburg

Fort
Atkinson

Genesee
Depot

Franklin

New
Glarus

90

Milton

43

94

Monroe

Delavan

Lake Geneva

Racine

Beloit

Clinton

Kenosha

SOUTHEAST

SOUTHEAST

The southeast part of Wisconsin is the part seen first by people fleeing Chicago on I-90 on Friday afternoon. Some of them pull over at the first opportunity and check in for the weekend, positioning themselves to be first in line for the trip back home on Sunday. More adventurous ones press on to places that at first must sound positively rustic— Spring Green, New Glarus, Mt. Horeb—but turn out to offer some of Wisconsin's best-known curiosities.

Wisconsin's largest city, Milwaukee, is in the southeast section. With a population of 600,000, the city has described itself as "Chicago several million people ago"—relatively affordable and maneuverable, right smack on Lake Michigan, and with its fair share of fancy architecture, including a bodacious art museum. Never mind that the curiosities described in this section seem to harken back to Milwaukee's days of beer and bowling.

The second-largest city is Madison, an island in a sea of reality—if you are to believe the T-shirts—a Brigadoon. It is the capital of Wisconsin and the home of the university and—come to think of it—a *radio* comedy-quiz show with a *live* audience that broadcasts all over the country on Saturday morning. Talk about your curiosities!

HONEY (THAT'S WHAT I WANT)
Ashippun

The Honey Museum asks the question that many bees would ask had they the time: Where would we be without bees?

I'm not saying that our lives would be impoverished without them, but besides all the wonderful pollination work they do, they give us Crayolas, moustache wax, lipstick, teat dilators, Ukrainian Easter-egg designs, and the little sheets you bite down on for the dentist, above and beyond honey. The Egyptians put honey in tombs for life in the hereafter, and Henry VIII signed all his official documents with a beeswax seal. And that's just two examples.

That's not all, as you shall learn at the museum at Honey Acres. When a bee finds a food source within 50 meters (54 yards), the bee does the *round dance* in quick short steps and runs in circles as other bees crowd around. When food is found more than 50 meters away, the bee does the *wag-tail dance*, and the more rapid the tail wagging, the more exciting the find. If the food is right on the border between 50 and 50-plus, he does the Watusi.

The statistics are awesome. Honeybees must visit two million flowers to gather enough nectar for one pound of honey. If he thought about it beforehand, he probably wouldn't do it: One bee collects only a tenth of a pound of honey in its entire lifetime, and that goes to the queen. It takes many, many bees flying a total of 25,000 miles to produce one pound of honey—that's equal to once around the world. Let's see sugar say that. How proud we can be of the honeybee, the Official State Insect.

It takes one Diehnelt family five generations of beekeeping to produce one honey of a museum. It is located 12 miles north

of I–94 on Highway 67, 2 miles north of Ashippun. Products
are for sale in the shop. Free admission to the museum. Open
9:00 A.M. to 3:30 P.M. Monday through Friday year-round; noon
to 4:00 P.M. Saturday and Sunday from May 15 through October 30. Call (920) 474–4411 for more information.

T OUCHED B Y AN E XHIBIT
B e l o i t

Many of the host of angels at the Angel Museum are made
of porcelain or wood, but some are also constructed from
drinking straws, tin-can lids, fur, coal, flower petals, or pasta
shells (that's a rigatoni body, bow-tie wings, macaroni arms).
The angels sing, fly, nap, leapfrog, sew, knit, sweep, fish,
marry, jitterbug, and play musical instruments. They wear
robes, halos, raincoats, and cheeseheads.

Some function as music boxes, cookie jars, or banks. Some
are very small; the second-smallest is an angel-shaped pewter
cookie cutter for a dollhouse. There are sets of angels for
each day of the week and month of the year. A set of nested
angels painted green, pink, and purple is a rarity from Rus-
sia. The museum also houses the black angel collection of
Oprah Winfrey.

The 6,000 pieces in the museum represent only about half
of the collection of Lowell and Joyce Berg. It all began one day
in 1976 when they went into an antiques store in Florida and
came out with two angel figurines. The following Christmas
they noticed several angels among their decorations and
decided to collect angels as souvenirs when they traveled.
Apparently they traveled a lot, because after that "it just snow-
balled," says Joyce, who usually wears a silver angel costume
with wings as she shows visitors around the museum.

From exit 185 on I–90 (at the landmark 40-foot can of chili with beans at the Hormel plant), go west on Highway 81 for about 3 miles, then turn south at the Rock River and look for the red brick church with round windows at 656 Pleasant Street. Open 10:00 A.M. to 4:00 P.M. Tuesday through Saturday; also open 1:00 to 4:00 P.M. Sunday, June through August; closed in January. Gift shop. Admission charge. For more information call (608) 362–9099 or check out www.angelmuseum.com.

A TRUCK OF ONE'S OWN
Clinton

About ten years ago Mark Madson converted a pickup truck—a 1959 Chevy Fleetside—into a tree house, with help from a buddy with a crane. "For fifteen bucks and a case of beer," says Madson, he hoisted it into a 30-foot tree.

What a swell clubhouse it turned out to be! It can hold as many as nine guys for beer and pizza. It's also a secluded spot for a date on Saturday night, if the woman is a good climber.

To keep the weight centered, Mark removed the engine and transmission. He also dumped five tons of dirt around the base of the tree and bolted the truck to the branches. He especially likes being up there in a windstorm. "It kind of creaks," he says. "It's cool because it rocks and rolls." He was there in 1996 when a tornado came through with 60 mph winds that blew the roof off his shed down below. What a ride!

None of this comes as a great surprise to family and friends who remember that when Mark was in seventh grade he took the engine off a lawn mower, put it in his bicycle, and left home for a week. Over the years many more projects followed. They usually combined engines, something tall, and maybe

Mark's cool clubhouse.

flames. A few years ago he almost invented the world's biggest weather vane, but it evolved into an artistic auto drop.

The truck in the tree is located 8 miles east of Beloit on the north side of I–43 just before the number 6 exit for Clinton. What Mark does next is anybody's guess. Keep posted at www.harleyheartbeat.com.

THE COW
THAT ROARED

We wuz robbed: Wisconsin is only a shadow of its former self.

In a lumber swindle instigated by wealthy New Englanders prior to Wisconsin's admittance to the Union in 1848, the land between the St. Croix and the Mississippi Rivers, including some choice parcels known as Minneapolis and St. Paul, a good chunk of northern Illinois ranging from Rock Falls to Chicago, and all of what should be known as the Upper Peninsula of Wisconsin, were stripped away from the state. We coulda been a contender, rivaling California and New York in electoral votes and general clout.

The insult to Badger pride was so great that Wisconsin actually seceded from the union in 1843, only nobody noticed. Under the dotty James Doty, territorial governor, Wisconsin declared itself to be a sovereign and independent (and thereby eligible for foreign aid) state ready to defend its integrity and citizenry—in effect, declaring war on the United States of America. This remains the only American war in which no skirmishes were fought, unless it was the one in Congress that caused Doty to be transferred to Utah, where it was thought he could do little harm. As in the South, some resentment remains to this day.

WISCONSIN DISCOVERS COLUMBUS
Columbus

A huge old brick building houses not only Wisconsin's largest antiques mall but also a museum dedicated to the city's namesake, Christopher Columbus, who, although he never visited Wisconsin, would have liked it here. The large collection of Columbus images includes not only plates, busts, and posters, but also many souvenirs from the World's Columbian Exposition of 1893, which honored his discovery of the New World some 400 years earlier.

The many depictions of the bearded man in mini-bloomers against a backdrop of ocean and ships make it easy to guess what the Exposition's souvenir floaty pens might have looked like. But plastic was not yet on the horizon, so the souvenirs instead are substantial and sometimes quaint items made of metal, paper, and cloth—thimbles, hairpin cases, handkerchiefs, watch-case openers, ice-cream molds, and much more. An especially impressive non sequitur is a model of the world's first Ferris wheel, which debuted at the Exposition. It was 250 feet high (nearly as high as the capitol in Madison), and its brave passengers rode in thirty-six enclosed cars, sixty in each, for a total of 2,160 people, many more than the *Niña*, the *Pinta*, and the *Santa Maria* combined.

An exhibit in the quincentenary department tells the story of a man who drove 30,000 miles photographing every community in the United States that was ever named Columbus, even if a tree out in the middle of a field was all that was left of it. That is the spirit that settled this great land of ours.

Columbus may be out of favor in many places, but not in Columbus.

Columbus Antique Mall and Christopher Columbus
Museum, 239 Whitney Street, about 2 blocks from the center
of the business district. Open 8:15 A.M. to 4:00 P.M. daily. Call
(920) 623–1992 for more information.

You Scratch My Bank
Columbus

A cross the street from a St. Vincent de Paul store and next
door to an abandoned bakery stands the Louis
Sullivan–designed Farmers
and Merchants Union Bank.
By the 1920s, when more
peas were canned in Columbus, Wisconsin, than any-
where else in the world, the
old bank had outlived the
telephone building. It was
time to build.

Naturally the bank
president at first thought
along the lines of Greek
classical. But for his wife,
no ordinary bank would
do. She had seen pho-
tographs of Sullivan
banks and was
impressed. The "father

*He thought Greek classical,
she thought Louis Sullivan.*

of the skyscraper" was summoned, he stayed, he designed. More history and description—tendrils, lintels, and all—are at www.fmub.com.

The bank is at 159 West James Street. Lobby opens at 9:00 A.M. and closes at 3:00 P.M. Monday through Thursday, at 5:30 P.M. Friday, and at 11:00 A.M. Saturday. The mezzanine has a small museum. Call (920) 623–4000 for information.

C L O N I N G   A R O U N D   A T   *A B S*
D e   F o r e s t

A BS (American Breeders Service) Global is known to dairy-men worldwide for its leadership in artificial insemination of cattle—and to Wisconsin motorists on I–90/94 for the puns on its billboard at company headquarters (OUR WIT IS A PLAY ON SEMENTICS, explained one).

ABS GENETICS IMPROVE YOUR DAIRY-HEIR. ABS THE CHAMPAGNE OF BOTTLED BULL. ABS IS THE CATTLE-ACT OF THE A.I. INDUSTRY. OUR BEST ASSETS ARE FROZEN. CALL US WHEN YOUR HEIFER'S IN THE MOOED. QUALITY GENETICS—MORE THAN A COWINCIDENT. LET ABS PUT A SMILE ON YOUR COW-TENANTS. MANY ARE CALLED BUT FEW ARE FROZEN. OUR GENES DON'T FADE. WE DELIVER THE MALE. They just keep coming.

ABS Global is also known for producing the world's first cloned calf (named Gene, of course) in 1997, just six months after Scotland announced the clonation of the sheep Dolly (GENETIC PROGRESS IS ALL RELATIVE). By now ABS has a herd of cloned cows.

ABS was founded in 1941, at first employing the delivery technique pictured on page 129, and the company shows signs of staying in business FOR HEIFER AND HEIFER. In 1999 ABS merged with a British company to form the largest artificial-insemination company in the world. WITH ABS MORE PROFIT IS IN THE BAG.

The bullboard is on the east side of I–90/94 between Highway V (exit 126) and Highway 19 (exit 131). For more bovine news see www.absglobal.com.

County Highway V offers two startling sights. To the west a life-size, flamingo-pink elephant wearing glasses looks down on interstate traffic from the Phillips 66 gas station and minimart. To the east a larger-than-life Holstein welcomes visitors to Ehlenbach's Cheese Chalet.

ROMEO AND JULIET
Delavan

Delavan was the home of twenty-six different circus companies in the 1800s, and the elephant that stands on a monument downtown in Tower Park is a facsimile of a rogue elephant, Romeo, who lived here between 1854 and 1865. One of the largest Indian elephants ever exhibited in America, he stood nearly 11 feet tall and weighed 10,500 pounds. In his day Romeo crushed, tusked, trampled, or otherwise killed five handlers. One time he escaped from his barn and terrorized the area for three days until captured.

An elephant named Juliet was from the same herd, imported from Ceylon (modern-day Sri Lanka) in 1851 for the P. T. Barnum Asiatic Caravan. Juliet was as delightful as Romeo was dangerous. She pulled a bandwagon in street parades, performed in the ring, and generally charmed her trainers.

Because she died in the month of February, in 1864, when the ground was frozen, Juliet's body was weighted down and deposited through a large rectangular hole sawed in the ice of Lake Delavan. In May 1897 a man trolling for northern pike off Lake Lawn reeled in part of a rib cage thought to have

CAN I USE YOUR CARMEX?

*T*he garage in Franklin, Wisconsin, where alchemist Alfred Woelbing first concocted Carmex in a ceramic warlock's pot has been demolished, but you can still tour the plant to watch molten lip balm poured into the diminutive white jars of mythic proportions. You just can't get too close to the production line, as the secrets of the process are a closely held family secret. Woelbing was the active president of the company until 2001, when he died at age one hundred (perhaps Carmex cures the ravages of age as well as cold sores). His son and grandsons continue company tradition.

While many believe that Carmex use caused the sixties, it really was invented in 1936 and may therefore have caused the thirties, forties, and fifties as well (although the Second World War disrupted grease availability, the core of the product). Carmex, perhaps because of comedian Paula Poundstone's "Carmex addict" routines, is reported to contain an addictive agent (some suggest fiberglass or an acid that causes an itch continually needing to be soothed); but it is, as far as we can tell, mostly wax, camphor, alum, menthol, and a little salicylic acid thrown in for analgesic properties. This does not assuage the conspiracy-laden Web sites (check out www.urbanlegends.com/ products).

Since 1987 Carmex has also come in little tubes, but it's just not the same. Long-term addicts claim the mere sound of the tiny jar opening provides relief from a host of symptoms, including but not limited to chapped derma.

belonged to Juliet, and in 1931 a drag-line operation yielded a tibia. Presumably the rest of her bones are still on the bottom of the lake. Romeo died in Chicago in 1892 after surgery for a foot infection, but the month was June, the weather was warm, and his remains were disposed of in the municipal dumping grounds.

DAIRY SHRINE / HOARD MUSEUM
Fort Atkinson

William Dempster Hoard taught the gospel of dairy farming. The National Dairy Shrine, within the Hoard Historical Museum, exhibits such relics as cow clippers, tail holders, glass milk bottles with their little cardboard lids, butterfat testers, cream separators, and even a dog-powered butter churn.

Representing modern technology is a photo exhibit that details today's method of artificial insemination of dairy cattle, from collection to next generation. It makes another item on exhibit seem especially touching: the parachute that dropped semen from the air to breeders down below before the advent of frozen semen. It looks like a little silk parasol, and its precious package is wrapped in discreet plain brown paper (Hoard had great respect for cows and was well known for saying that one should "Speak to a cow as you would a lady"). A photograph of a very small plane, the *Flying Bull*, and its barnstorming pilot completes the picture.

The Hoard Historical Museum has artifacts from the Black-hawk War; hundreds of arrowheads handsomely displayed; many mounted birds, including a passenger pigeon; and a horseskin rug with mane.

Artificial insemination of cattle used to be a chancy business. Sometimes the parachute that delivered the goods, like this one at the National Dairy Shrine, blew into the next county.

Located on Whitewater Avenue (Highway 12 East) in Fort Atkinson. Open 9:30 A.M. to 3:30 P.M. Tuesday through Saturday, and 1:00 to 5:00 P.M. on the first Sunday of the month from September through May; 9:30 A.M. to 4:30 P.M. Tuesday through Saturday, and 11:00 A.M. to 3:00 P.M. Sunday in June, July, and August. No hours on Monday, ever. Call (920) 563–7769 for more details.

Rick Serocki sawed a purple 1955 Fleetwood Cadillac in half and planted it in his front yard in Cudahy. Its bumper sticker says, IF WE CAN'T FIX IT, WE'LL BURY IT—MILWAUKEE BODY SHOP.

FLOSSIE'S BEST FRIEND

If Wisconsin does have more cows than people, it is only because they are encouraged to breed. And encouraging them to breed is the legacy of William D. Hoard of Fort Atkinson. Hoard was one of the first to speak of "cow temperament," something the rest of us in Dairyland have come to take for granted as a birthright.

Around the turn of the last century, Hoard wrote the dairy commandments:

Speak to a cow as you would to a lady.

Remember that a cow is a mother and her calf is a baby.

To him that loveth a cow, shall all other things be added—

feed, ensilage, butter, more grasses, more prosperity,

happier homes and greater wealth.

Hoard promoted the radical notions of the single-purpose milker; the building of silos; the testing of milk to protect against tuberculosis; and, in fact, transformed the farm in which several cows were kept into the modern dairy industry and the landscape of Wisconsin into the beautiful patchwork of dairy farms and fields you see today. Along the way he served in the Civil War; was elected governor of the state (as a Republican and Lincoln disciple, although ridiculed as the "cow candidate"); promoted the planting of alfalfa; brought Ag Science to the University of Wisconsin; made the farmer a political force to be reckoned with nationally; and founded Hoard's Dairyman, *the influential journal still published today.*

A statue of Hoard stands at the head of the agricultural campus at the University of Wisconsin–Madison, where you will want to be sure to stop at Babcock Hall to sample the ice cream and visit the dairy barns.

TEN CHIMNEYS
Genesee Depot

For decades Alfred Lunt and Lynn Fontanne were America's "First Couple" of the theater, and when they finished a long run on Broadway they came home to Genesee Depot. Here they could roam the fields or play host to all their theatrical friends. Helen Hayes stayed here for a month or so every year. Eugene O'Neill worked on *Strange Interlude*. Noel Coward played the piano (and painted pictures all over it). Many others came and went—Charlie Chaplin, Laurence Olivier, Carol Channing, Katharine Hepburn, Julie Harris, Alexander Woollcott, S. N. Behrman, Robert Sherwood, Moss Hart—all right here in the rural hamlet of Genesee Depot.

Lunt had grown up in Milwaukee and loved the Wisconsin countryside. Over the years he acquired land, converted a chicken coop into a summer cottage, and added buildings whose chimneys numbered ten and gave the estate its name. Lunt was serious about his land. He grew strawberries, raspberries, tomatoes, cucumbers, turnips, potatoes, and corn. He made his own butter and bred cattle.

"The Fabulous Lunts" designed every room in the main house like a stage set, fit for grand entrances and exits. A set designer covered the walls and ceilings with elaborate murals. In one scene from the Old Testament, Adam and Eve resemble each other because Fontanne posed for both. Fond of old things, she said, "Being in a modern house all the rest of my life would be just like sitting nude forever in the center of a huge white dinner plate." Artwork and antiques from New York and Europe fill the rooms.

Lunt and Fontanne were married for fifty-five years. Lunt died in 1977, and Fontanne stayed on at Ten Chimneys until she died in 1983. It had been their permanent home since 1972, their summer retreat since the 1920s.

In 2003, after a multimillion-dollar restoration, Ten Chimneys was opened to the public as a museum and arts center. Tours are offered from 10:00 A.M. to 2:45 P.M. Tuesday through Saturday, April through October. Admission charge. Reservations are a good idea. Call (262) 968–4110. Prepare to be dazzled.

Bells Bells Bells Bells Bells Bells Bells
Germantown

*B*ells for horses, sheep, water buffalo, elephants, turkeys, dogs, babies, sleighs, bikes, and the Salvation Army. Bells that look like turtles, seahorses, Santa Claus, Charlie Chaplin, King Arthur, Little Miss Muffett, and Clara Barton. Bells made of brass, pottery, bisque, copper. Bells from every country. Bell-things that dial rotary phones in India and bells that signal a fisherman that he's got a bite. Bells for more reasons than you ever imagined. Even hell's bells might be here.

The bells belonged to Sila Lydia Bast, who grew up nearby and found her first bell, a cow bell, in a field not far from here. She started a collection and word got around. When she worked with her family in the Little Gem Restaurant in Milwaukee, customers brought her bells. Later she became a world traveler and collected more bells. The bells started to add up. Before all was said and done, the Swiss had cast a cow bell especially in her honor. Talk about your tintinnabulation!

Bast Bell Museum is 2 miles east of Highway 41/45 (Holy Hill exit). Open 11:00 A.M. to 4:00 P.M. Tuesday through Sunday, April to November, year-round by appointment. Admission charge. Call (262) 628–3170. Before you leave, take a look in the next room at a very spiffy 1929 fire truck.

A flying saucer at rest on County Highway D north of Belleville, where several UFO sightings were reported in the 1970s. This one has a hatchway and running lights.

FINALLY, AN OUTLET STORE FOR GUYS
Kenosha

There's no need for Dad to doze off in the parking lot at Prime Outlets while Mom and Sis are going nuts inside Donna Karan and J. Crew. Just on the other side of I–94 is the Kenosha Military Museum, an outdoor display of heavy equipment from World War I through Desert Storm—tanks, helicopters, landing craft . . . vehicles of all kinds in khaki tones.

The most conspicuous item is the huge Sky Crane, a heavy-lift helicopter that transported equipment in the Vietnam War. You can get behind the wheel of a Humvee, a fast-attack vehicle, or a helicopter for a hands-on but stationary experience or photo op.

Some vehicles are for sale, and some are for rent if you're Steven Spielberg (landing craft and weapons carrier in *Saving Private Ryan*) or Denzel Washington (British Centurions dressed up like Abrams tanks in *Courage under Fire*). And if you don't see what you're looking for on the lot, the gift shop sells catalogs that can help make a dream of a Sherman tank in your driveway come true.

Open from 9:00 A.M. to 5:00 P.M. Wednesday through Saturday, 10:00 A.M. to 5:00 P.M. Sunday year-round, except in inclement weather. Located on the frontage road, County Q, about a mile south of Highway 165 at I–94 (exit 374). Admission charge. Call (262) 857–3418 for details.

In 1910 Cooper Underwear Company patented its Kenosha Klosed Krotch long underwear, and the following year it became the first underwear manufacturer to advertise in national magazines. In 1972 the Kenosha company changed its name to Jockey International.

In about 1862, when John Muir was a student at the University of Wisconsin, he invented a desk that awoke him by collapsing his bed and lighting a lamp. The desk gave him a few minutes to get dressed, and then it opened the first book he planned to study, whisked it away at the allotted time, opened the next book, and kept this up until he'd read all his assignments. The desk is about 9 feet tall, has legs whittled into the shapes of little books, and is on display on the main floor of the Wisconsin Historical Society in Madison. John Muir became famous as a naturalist and conservationist.

GAWKING AND WALKING
Lake Geneva

Lake Geneva is one of the few places in the country that still delivers mail by boat, and the boat seems to be the only one that invites passengers to come aboard and watch the show. See the postal person leap off the boat, scamper across the pier, shove the mail in the box, race back with the outgoing mail in her teeth, and leap onto the rail of the 75-foot *Walworth II*, which never stopped! Everybody cheers!

But there's more. Those piers are attached not to cottages but to grandiose estates. As you shall hear (between deliveries, the mail-jumper demonstrates that she can read fast, too), many of these mansions were originally built by captains of Chicago-area industries: brewing, chewing gum, meat packing, railroads, department stores, hotels, pianos, bicycles, washing machines— everything from salt to barbed wire. Who'd have thought there was so much money in paper caps for milk bottles? A lot, if you invented them, as Olaf Tevander did and then retired to that chalet-style mansion at age twenty-six. (You may remember seeing his bottle caps at the National Dairy Shrine, p. 128). There's Otto Young's place. He started out selling jewelry from a pushcart and ended up building the largest house on the lake, approximately the size of Xanadu. Another imposing manor was built under a circus tent so that A. C. Bartlett—that old sweetie!—could surprise his wife on her birthday.

Curiosities include a four-story guest house that's a fully operational lighthouse, a la the Cape Elizabeth Light in Maine. The occupants of the house on Duck Island have to park at the country club and complete the commute by golf cart. For obvious reasons, the *Walworth II* skips the pier with the steep one-hundred-step staircase leading from the lake to the front

A mail jumper in action.

terrace. These folks pick up their mail at the road, as others choose to do, though some must endure a long schlep down the driveway.

If you want to check out the architecture, the landscaping, or the lamp in the picture window at closer range, you can take a walk-and-gawk self-tour, which allows you to tromp right across the front lawns of these grand estates. The property is private, but the path is public. Note that the yard art tends more toward iron ibis than plastic flamingo, and the lawn furniture . . . but hey, the chairs I bought at Target look as good as those! Hear the *pooka-pooka* of their tennis balls in the distance. Mostly the occupants are invisible. Probably inside, writing checks.

The mail boat departs at 9:45 A.M. daily, June 15 through
September 15, from Riviera Docks, a block south of the main
downtown intersection of Broad Street (Highway 120) and
Main Street (Highway 50) in Lake Geneva (the town). The trip
around Geneva Lake (the lake) lasts about two and a half
hours. Admission charge. You can purchase the Geneva Lake
Shore Path guide, called *Walk, Talk, and Gawk,* at several
locations in town, or send $7.50 to P.O. Box 413, Lake Geneva,
WI 53147. The guide includes maps, breaks down the 21-mile
path into seven segments, and offers highlights and history.

A P Y R A M I D S C H E M E ?
L a k e M i l l s

L ake Mills owes its nickname, the "City of Pyramids" (and
such local businesses as the Pyramid Driving School), to
three mysterious shapes at the bottom of Rock Lake.

In the nineteenth century Winnebagoes were telling the
early European settlers of Lake Mills about sunken "rock
tepees," and one day in 1900 two local duck hunters peered
down and saw them. Over the years fishermen and divers have
reported sighting something—and described an upside-down
ice-cream cone, or a Hershey's Chocolate Kiss, 20 or 30 feet
high and 100 feet long—but most of the time water conditions
have defied even high-tech video equipment. Are they man-made
or glacial debris? Some believe that pre-Columbian dwellers built
them on dry land before the area was flooded. Others say that
geology can explain the whole thing. The question remains:
archaeological find of the century, or nature at work?

Those in the pyramid-builder camp point to large, flat-
topped pyramidal mounds a few miles east of Lake Mills.
Archaeologists say that the people who lived here between

about A.D. 900 and 1200 built the mounds, plus a stockade of wooden posts around their village. One mound had fire pits lined with sand; another was for burials; a third was used for storing corn. Portions of the stockade and two mounds have been reconstructed at Aztalan State Park.

The unexplained underwater shapes are at the south end of Rock Lake. The archaeological site is within Aztalan State Park and is listed in the National Register of Historic Places. The park is located south of I–94 (exit 259) and is open daily from April through October.

ANCIENT FOSSILS IN THE CAPITOL
Madison

The yellow marble walls of the Hearing Room in the State Capitol Building contain dozens of ammonites, from the days when the future capitol site was sunk in a seventy-million-year-old sea and giant snails made backroom deals. The ancient fossils look just like big snails.

You don't have to wait for a hearing on some burning issue to see them. Most of the time the Hearing Room is unoccupied, and you're welcome to go in and look around. The ammonites are at eye level, and some of them are as large as 8 inches across.

When you leave the Hearing Room, head down the right side of the grand staircase and admire the starfish fossil on the fourth step from the bottom. It's about 400 million years old, and geologists say it's extremely rare. (Starfish lack the rigid skeleton necessary for preservation as fossils.)

At the bottom of the staircase, bear right toward the west wing and walk down the grand staircase to the ground floor. To the right of the bottom step is a cephalopod, about 20 inches long. This creature too is about 400 million years old; it lived in the sea, and, like the ammonite, had a hard body but a straight one, not coiled. You can see the breathing tube that ran down the length of its shell—it inhaled to sink, exhaled to rise. If you cross the rotunda to the south wing, you can see another cephalopod, or a chunk of one, on the floor between the two drinking fountains near the elevator on the east side.

The Hearing Room is in the north wing, second floor. Free guided tours of this glorious building are offered daily. Large groups should make an online reservation at www.wisconsin .gov/state/captour or call (608) 266–0382. On a scale of one to ten, say state capitol junkies, this one is an eleven.

C o w s   o n   t h e   C a m p u s
M a d i s o n

There's a strange sight at the Dairy Cattle Instruction and Research Center at the University of Wisconsin—cows with portholes in their sides. It's in the interest of science, a means of observing digestive processes. The cows don't appear to mind, and the dairy-science people assure us that they don't.

If you get up bright and early or stop by the center late in the afternoon, you can stand at a big picture window and watch cows being milked. Then, if you ask, you can go backstage and look for the cows with the portholes. If you're lucky, maybe someone with a good reason to want to know what's going on in there will come along, remove the plug-style porthole, reach inside, and pull out some stomach contents.

The Dairy Research Center is at 1815 Linden Drive, just a few doors down from the busy Babcock Dairy Store, which sells ice cream, cheese, and butter made from the milk of these very cows.

JEFFERSONIAN DEMOCRACY

Thomas Jefferson never made it to Wisconsin (although his exploratory committee—Lewis, Clark, and Sacajawea—made it darn close). But his youngest son by Sally Hemings, his household slave at Monticello, did.

Eston Hemings Jefferson is buried in Madison's Forest Hills cemetery (on Speedway Road), along with his wife, Julia, and eight family members. Eston was the scion of a successful and well-respected Madison family that ran the Capital Hotel, a livery business that was active in early union associations. Recently DNA testing provided evidence that Eston's father was one of the Founding Fathers. Jefferson never formally freed his slaves but purportedly agreed to allow many to run away.

In 1836, at age twenty-eight, Eston fled to Ohio, and when the political tide turned against former slaves with the passage of the Fugitive Slave Act, he moved to the freshly minted state of Wisconsin in 1851. He married a black woman but lived as a white man, concealing his family history to his death in 1856. His brother Madison, who lived in Ohio, claimed the lineage to Jefferson in a biography and mentioned a brother in Wisconsin, though not by name, for his brother's well-being.

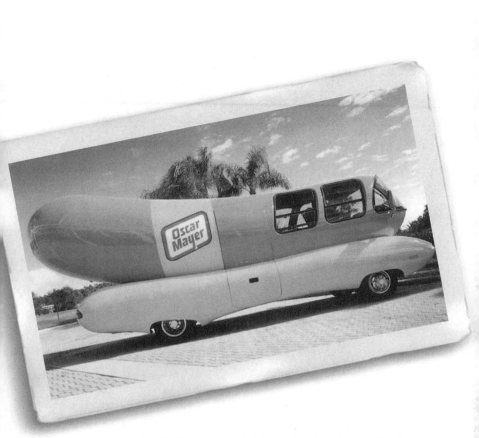

The 27-foot Wienermobile has a hot dog–shaped glove box
and instrument panel, relish-colored seats, and storage space for up to
10,000 wiener whistles. Drivers of the six-wiener fleet are usually recent college graduates who must train at Hot Dog High in Madison, the home of
Oscar Mayer Foods, before they get the keys to the five-ton wiener.

The Dreamkeepers, two 35-foot birds, offer a unique landmark for the occupants of 211 South Paterson in Madison. They were created by Dr. Evermor of Baraboo (see page 186) who loves birds "because they are the most nonthreatening species on our planet." As usual, he used industrial scrap: parts from a semi that tipped over in Indiana, two large blowers, and many scissors blades. The Dreamkeepers also have intergalactic names: Yon and Beyond.

ENTOMOLOGIZER AND CRICKET SPITTER
Madison

Dan Capps holds the world's record in cricket spitting. First he won the Bug Bowl Cricket-Spitting Contest at Purdue University, where he was exhibiting his insect collection. Then, to satisfy Guinness's tough standards, he repeated the deed on its *World Records Prime Time* television show in Hollywood. His official distance is 32 feet ½ inch.

A competition cricket is dead, limp, and mushy, having been frozen and thawed.

Dan's personal insect collection contains tens of thousands of insects—wasps, beetles, moths, butterflies, dragonflies, and, of course, crickets—with an emphasis on tropical species. It's an enormous collection for an amateur (he earns his livelihood as a mechanic at Oscar Mayer). Dan's knowledge of insects is self-taught, and he often shows and talks about wonders of the insect world at schools and elsewhere. (His own fascination with insects began in grade school when the principal opened a cigar box and showed Dan his luna and cecropia moths.) Dan sees his school visits as a chance to open eyes to diversity in nature and to enlighten—people who shriek at the sight of an insect the size of a baseball, for instance, learn that large insects often are harmless. A well-respected collector, he also gets invitations to address entomologists' professional meetings.

Dan's own person further testifies to the significance of ecology in his life. Two artist friends designed a tapestry of images from nature—his favorite butterflies, insects, and flowers—that is tattooed over his upper body (but it doesn't extend below his elbows—that is, the tattoo insects won't freak out the school principal at his "Introduction to Insects" visits at grade schools).

For more information write or call Dan Capps at P.O. Box 8216, Madison, WI 53708, (608) 332–5434.

GOOD GRIEF
Middleton

*S*am Sanfillippo displays his enormous collection of taxidermied wildlife downstairs at the funeral home that bears his name. It takes four large rooms here to contain the hundreds of fish, birds, and animals he has hunted or otherwise acquired, and there are more at home. As a teenager he caught the gigantic marlin on the wall, which is almost eclipsed by all that followed.

He and his personal Northwoods taxidermist obviously have had fun dreaming up settings for subjects. At the "Woodland Fair," several chipmunks ride a merry-go-round, while others in skirts of gold upholstery fringe perform at the "topless girlie show." Albino squirrels shoot baskets at a Fisher-Price hoop or pose in shocking-pink convertibles. Gray squirrels line up for refills at a Northwoods bar.

Interesting stories are behind many of the acquisitions. The wild boar charged out of the brush in the backwoods of Georgia. The two tiny fawns were found inside a doe that had been hit by a car. The albino squirrels came from a park in St. Louis. The three-legged goose, the blonde raccoons, and the paddle-nosed catfish are rarities.

Photographs of Sanfillippo with presidents, governors, and astronauts offer another dimension of his long and full life. And the animals speak for themselves.

Visitors are welcome, but call first: (608) 238–8406. Sanfillippo Cress Funeral Home is at 6021 University Avenue.

One-stop shopping on Winnequah Road in Madison.

A SECRET TUNNEL
Milton

J oseph Goodrich was an innkeeper, a devout Seventh Day
Baptist, and such a staunch abolitionist that he dug a
50-foot tunnel between his log cabin and his inn to aid fugitive
slaves as they traveled the Underground Railroad to freedom.
When runaways found their way to the cabin, Goodrich lifted
the secret trapdoor to the secret tunnel that led to the secret
room in the basement. There they could hide and rest up for
the next leg of the perilous journey.

The Underground Railroad of the
nineteenth century was not, of
course, a real railroad, and this
seems to be the only part of it that
actually was underground.

The inn was Milton House, and
upstairs from the secret room,
guests were resting up after a hard
day's stagecoach ride. Sojourner Truth
was once a guest, and although she and

*Grout
fanciers may be
interested to know that
Milton House is the oldest
poured-grout structure
in the United
States.*

Goodrich saw eye to eye on abolition, they disagreed on smoking. Sojourner Truth smoked a pipe, and Goodrich told her that
she wouldn't get to heaven because smoking made her breath
bad. She said she wouldn't need her breath in heaven.

Goodrich was one of Milton's first settlers (and therefore
didn't have to worry about neighbors who might wonder why
he was digging that tunnel), having arrived in March 1839
with his family after a thirty-four-day trip by covered wagon
from Alfred, New York—a hotbed of the abolitionist movement.
He constructed the inn in 1844, and when it was finished, the

Janesville Gazette described it as "truly an object of curiosity." It was in the shape of a hexagon and had a chimney in the middle so that each room could have its own stove and stovepipe connection to the chimney.

In 1998 the National Park Service officially recognized the Milton House Museum as a National Historic Landmark for its role in the Underground Railroad. The museum is located at the intersection of Highways 26 and 59. Guided tours daily from 10:00 A.M. to 5:00 P.M. Memorial Day through Labor Day and weekends in May (tours by arrangement at other times of year). Admission charge. Call (608) 868–7772 or see www.miltonhouse.org for more information.

*A*rthur D. Hasler is credited with solving one of the great mysteries of salmon migration in 1945. As a professor of zoology at University of Wisconsin–Madison, he hypothesized that salmon use their sense of smell to find their way home. He proved it by collecting salmon, stuffing cotton up the noses of some of them, and sending them back downstream. The ones without the cotton found their way straight off; the ones with cotton got confused and made mistakes.

*Not a bird, not a plane—but the Milwaukee Art Museum, as if
ready to flap its wings and take off across Lake Michigan.
Architect Santiago Calatrava designed the Quadracci Pavilion
with wings forming a sunshade that opens and closes when the
museum opens and closes (10:00 A.M. to 5:00 P.M. daily, until
8:00 on Thursday), and also at noon.*

HOME OF THE OOF OOF POLKA
Milwaukee

A rt Altenburg yearned for a concertina when he was a boy. To help him earn the money, his father, a farmer, gave him a quarter acre of land. The number of rocks and roots that Art first had to clear out are forever engraved in his memory, but eventually he was able to grow and sell enough cucumbers to the local pickle factory to earn the $60 he needed for the concertina. Today he has fifty-eight concertinas (accordions with buttons for keys) at his Art Altenburg's Concertina Bar.

Art's place is actually a whole concertina universe, and hundreds come here on weekends for polka music and dancing. Bands play on Friday and Saturday nights, such as Karl and the Country Dutchmen from Minnesota or even Art's own Jolly Jacks Concertina Orchestra. He has composed a few numbers of his own, such as "The Oof Oof Polka." Locals turn up on Thursday nights for jam sessions.

There's no taxidermy in this bar. Instead, the walls are covered with brass instruments, photographs of polka bands and concertina players, and awards such as "Wisconsin Polka Entertainment Center Operator of the Year, 1994."

Art is sorry to say that the place is for sale, but he hopes it will continue as a concertina bar, the only one in the country. Art's Concertina Bar, 1920 South Thirty-seventh Street, off Burnham Avenue, opens at 11:00 A.M. weekdays. Closed Sunday. Music goes from 9:00 P.M. to 1:00 A.M. Friday, 9:00 P.M. to 1:30 A.M. Saturday. Call (414) 384–2570 for more details or see www.artsconcertinabar.net.

AND SOME REALLY ANCIENT PIN BOYS
Milwaukee

From the outside Holler House looks like about a thousand other corner taverns in Milwaukee, but beyond the door at the end of the bar and down the stairs is bowling history: the oldest alleys (all two of them) in the nation.

The American Bowling Congress sanctioned them in 1910, and they're very much in use today. See the bowling bags lined up in the "locker room"—two long shelves under the front window. Some regulars have been coming for forty years. Bowlers sacrifice fifteen or twenty points to play here. It's disorienting to bowl in a tunnel instead of a thirty-lane alleyrama, on hardwood instead of synthetic lanes, with balls that come rumbling back in full view from human pin setters busily scampering around back there.

Photos of bowling teams confirm the history—upstanding-looking guys wearing white shirts and neckties and representing Ryczek Embalmers, Miller High Life, La Dora Cigars. Fourth-generation owner Marcy Skowronski knows the neighborhood stories that go with them. She also can explain another feature of the Holler House decor: brassieres autographed by their owners, dangling in bunches from various fixtures.

Holler House, 2042 West Lincoln, opens for business at 4:00 P.M. every day except Monday. Call to inquire about bowling (414–647–9284), and watch for scenes filmed at Holler House in the movie *Chump Change*.

MILWAUKEE TALKING

*I*n Milwaukee *"Come by the house later"* does not mean
that the speaker is expecting you to make an offer on the
duplex, nor does it imply that the addressee will not be
invited in. It's just how you ask somebody over. Although if
you can't wait to be asked, you can still station yourself
under a friend's window and yell *"Call for Steve-ee!"* if, in
fact, it's Stevie you want to see.

Milwaukee's German argot (further complicated in
my family with Yiddish-isms) makes "bubblers" out of
drinking fountains, finds "icebox" still the preferred
term for refrigerator, and *"ain'a?"* the way to conclude
a declarative sentence. (*"Follow me?"* my dad's preferred
closer, is another favorite.)

While it may not be true that Milwaukee nearly entered
the war on the German side, "Cream City" syntax owes a lot
to loose—or literal—translations from the German and, on
the South Side, the Polish. Milwaukee Talk, a pamphlet originally published by the Milwaukee Journal in the 1950s (and
cited in James P. Leary's Wisconsin Folklore) is an invalu-
able primer for wannabe Milwaukeeans:

"It's warm in here. Why don't you run up the window?"
"From the refrigerator get the eggs and I will fry you."
"Don't nervous me, I get easy mad."
"Come broom off the snow, the sidewalk is getting thick."
"I gotta clean my hairs, they're so greasy."

Naturally, to poetry it lends itself:

> I give to you a violet
> In token of I'm glad we met
> I hope we may already yet
> Once more again together get.

So stop in at Goldmann's (p. 156) and have a coffee cup
and a pie slice.

REMEMBER TO FIRST GET YOUR
GRAPEFRUIT DRILLED
Milwaukee

If your bowling score suffered at Holler House, you'll feel a lot better about it at Koz's. According to comments in the visitors' book that Duwayne Kosakoski keeps at the bar, his customers are positively thrilled with the totals they rack up in the next room. It seems to help that the game here is miniature bowling. The four alleys are only 16 feet long, the pins are 9 inches high, and the ball is akin to a four-pound grapefruit.

At one time mini-bowling was a major pastime in Milwaukee; today Koz's offers the only game in town. "The most honest bowling in America is at Koz's Mini-Bowl," wrote Frank Deford in *Sports Illustrated*, where "almost anybody can bowl a 300. Many folks in the area do their bowling only at Koz's, because the company is good, the beer is cold, and there's hard truth enough in the rest of the world."

Bowling hours are not during school hours, because school kids set the pins; not Thursday, because that's league night for eight men's teams; and not when the Packers are playing on television. Travelers from all over the world have searched out Koz's Mini-Bowl and Bar and mixed with the neighborhood regulars at 2078 South Seventh Street (at Becher). Call (414) 383–0560 for more information.

*This house was built in 1926
from plans for a ship, by a salesman who dreamed of
sailing the high seas. White with blue trim and with a 30-foot lighthouse off the
starboard bow, the one-bedroom Edmund B is at the corner of North
Cambridge Avenue and East Hampshire Street, near the University of
Wisconsin–Milwaukee campus.*

JURASSIC RETAIL
Milwaukee

Goldmann's and Dretzka's department stores are two examples of the *Milwaukee Journal*'s statement in 1998 that "retro may be hot now but in Milwaukee it never went out of style." These stores seem to have changed hardly a whit in the past century.

Goldmann's is especially beloved for its World Famous Diner, which serves breakfast, lunch, and dinner at three U-shaped counters. Waitresses from central casting serve such classics as the Meatloaf Dinner and the Incredible Malt. Formica counter, chrome stools, and six-tier pie cases complete the picture.

Dretzka's has no lunch counter, but it has items that would be hard to find anywhere else: men's garters, jingle bells on cards, buttons in boxes, a wide selection of plastic rain bonnets—plain, with daisies, or with Wonder Bread dots. If you're looking for something specific in this large store, however, it would be wise to ask. You wouldn't think to look for the rubber chickens, for instance, between the insoles and the zippers, but that is where they are.

Goldmann's has merchandise, too—three floors of clothing and housewares and a mezzanine of colorful, kitschy lamps.

Goldmann's and Dretzka's are on the south side of Milwaukee. Goldmann's, 930 West Mitchell, is open weekdays at 9:00 A.M. and closes at 5:30 P.M. every day except Friday, when it closes at 8:00 P.M. It's also open from 11:00 A.M. to 4:00 P.M. the first Sunday of the month. Dretzka's, 4746 South Packard Avenue, Cudahy, is open 9:00 A.M. to 5:00 P.M. Monday through Saturday, closed Sunday.

WHY MILWAUKEE FEELS BADLY

*J*ohn Schrank, a bartender, convinced that Theodore Roosevelt intended to establish a monarchy by running for a third term, stalked him for 2,000 miles before putting a bullet in him in Milwaukee in 1912. It didn't help that William McKinley had appeared to him in a dream pointing to Roosevelt as McKinley's murderer—which, in Schrank's mind, was more portentous than just something he had eaten before retiring.

Fortunately for Roosevelt, the length of his speech may have saved his life. The bullet had to pass through the doubled-up bulk of a fifty-page speech as well as a case for the metal spectacles he needed to read it. In true Bull Moose fashion, he railed for an hour with the bullet lodged 5 inches into his chest, where, having missed all major organs and arteries, it was to remain for the rest of his life. Roosevelt said, "I don't want Milwaukee to feel badly about this," which has come to be the city's unofficial motto since October 14, 1912. Still, he was removed to Chicago's Mercy Hospital for treatment, even though Mt. Sinai was just down the street.

Teddy was actually shot leaving his hotel on the way to the Milwaukee Auditorium; it was on the ride there that an aide noticed the hole in the president's overcoat. Asking only for a clean handkerchief to stem the blood flow, Roosevelt launched into his stump speech, during which it became clear to his audience that something was dreadfully wrong.

Schrank was eventually confined to the Hospital for the Criminally Insane in Oshkosh, and Roosevelt lost his bid for a third term to Woodrow Wilson, suffering lifelong debilities from the wound (complicated by untreated malaria from a subsequent rafting trip in the Amazon; the man did not know from convalescing).

For years Milwaukee suffered image problems due to the assassination attempt. It had nearly recovered when a Milwaukee lad, Arthur Bremer, undid it all by shooting George Wallace in 1972.

One summer day in 1909, Ole Evinrude purchased ice cream for a picnic, but by the time he rowed across Okauchee Lake in Waukesha County to the picnic site, the sweet stuff had melted. His disappointment led to his inventing "the detachable rowboat motor" and organizing Evinrude Motor Company.

The tin man of Highway 78 awaits his friend the rural mail carrier. Farther down the driveway is 13-foot-high Peg Leg Pete, a pirate with rail spikes for teeth and a frying pan for an eye patch. Located about halfway between Black Earth and Mount Horeb.

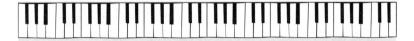

*L*iberace, *born Wladziu Valentino Liberace in West Allis, attended West Milwaukee High School, where he almost always won first prize for "Most Original Costume" on Character Day. At various times he was Haile Selassie, Yankee Doodle Dandy, and Greta Garbo. At age fourteen he presented his first piano recital at Wisconsin College of Music, and at twenty he soloed with the Chicago Symphony Orchestra, under the name Walter Buster Keys.*

S T I N K S   S O   G O O D
M o n r o e

C halet Cheese Co-op is the only factory in this country that makes the notoriously funky-smelling Limburger. Fifty years ago about one hundred plants made Limburger, but tastes change, and now Chalet Cheese stands alone.

The Chalet Cheese Co-op doesn't offer tours, T-shirts, or tasting parties. It does, however, have a store that sells its products (Limburger, brick, and baby Swiss). In an adjoining room you can see the decidedly low-tech, labor-intensive packaging operation: three or four women in white seated at a table wrapping little blocks of Limburger in rectangles of parchment paper, then waxed paper, and finally foil. The one million pounds of Limburger they wrap annually are sold throughout the United States under various labels; so if you buy domestic limburger, it came from *here*.

The store is open from 6:00 A.M. to 3:30 P.M. Monday through Friday, 8:00 A.M. to 10:30 A.M. Saturday. Chalet Cheese Co-op is located at N4858 County Road N (a roller-coaster-style road) about 4 miles north of Monroe. Call (608) 325–4343 for more information.

Limburger is generally associated with practical jokes and sandwiches, and the best place to appreciate the latter—on buttered toast with a slice of sweet onion and a little honey—is Baumgartner's Tavern in Monroe. Baumgartner's believes there's not a place in the world that sells more Limburger sandwiches, and they always serve theirs with a mint. Further reminders of the area's Swiss heritage appear in the form of huge oil paintings of alpine scenes; nearly half a mountain goat, among other hunting trophies; and local guys playing cards—as well as a photo of Miss Limburger of 1998 in a recent Cheese Days parade.

Baumgartner's Cheese Store and Tavern is on the west side of the Green County Courthouse Square. Hours are 8:00 A.M. to bar time, seven days a week. Call (608) 325–6157 for details.

GOT MUSTARD?
Mount Horeb

The night in 1986 that the Boston Red Sox lost the World Series, Wisconsin's Assistant Attorney General Barry Levenson was distraught. Seeking comfort in food, he went to an all-night supermarket and had an epiphany in the condiment aisle: "When I stood before the mustards, a voice spoke to me: 'If you collect us, they will come.'"

The collection began in the basement of his home and moved to a pump house in the backyard. One Saturday morning several years later, with the help of a "Pass the Mustard" human chain, it was moved into a store a few blocks away on Main Street.

Today Barry is curator of the Mount Horeb Mustard Museum and dean of Poupon U, which offers six degrees, at $7.50 per diploma, from Ph.D. (Philosopher of Dijon) to J.D. (Juris Dufus). The museum has more than 4,000 jars of mustard from all fifty states and sixty countries, a fine display of antique mustard pots, mustard-in-music items, and many other things mustard. The Mustard Piece Theater runs the video *Mustard: The Spice of Nations.*

Annual events include a reunion of people named Mustard and National Mustard Day early in August. If nothing else, the Mustard Museum proves that you can promote anything.

Mount Horeb Mustard Museum, 100 West Main Street, is open from 10:00 A.M. to 5:00 P.M. daily. Give them a call at (800) 438–6878 or see www.mustardmuseum.com.

JA, DAS IST EINE DUNCE CAP
New Glarus

On May 13, 1845, two valleys' worth of villagers—fewer than 200 people in all—from the Swiss canton of Glarus said farewell to Europe forever and sailed for America. On June 18 they ran out of potatoes; on July 19—by now aboard a riverboat on the Ohio—they were attacked by bloodthirsty mosquitoes. But in Galena, Illinois, they were reunited with the advance guard, two men who had been sent to scout for a place comparable to home and found it in Green County, Wisconsin. Together they walked the last 60 miles.

The soil was rich, water was plentiful, the landscape sort of resembled Switzerland, and the price was right—$1.25 per acre. On July 17, 1845, they purchased 1,280 acres and called their new village New Glarus.

The Swiss Historical Village consists of fourteen buildings that tell the rest of the story. A family of eight lived in the authentic 14-by-16-foot log cabin. In the one-room church, they endured two-hour sermons. The 1880 general store displays standard merchandise as well as examples of what an irrepressible Swiss can do with a sharp knife: intricate memorials carved from beeswax, cathedral-like superstructures of wood, a necklace of fruit pits.

Among other heavy-duty equipment in the blacksmith shop is a *schnitzelbank*, the very one in question in the hearty drinking song that asks *"Ist das nicht eine schnitzelbank? Ja, das ist eine schnitzelbank . . ."* The fully equipped, original one-room *schul haus* even has a dunce cap—not just some flimsy cone-thing fashioned from a piece of notebook paper, but a sturdy, deadly serious dunce cap. The print shop has all the equipment needed to print the *New Glarus Post* and, among other news clips, Mrs. T. C. Hefty's 20-column-inch recipe for soap: "Dissolve one can Eagle brand lye in one quart of cold rain water . . ."

Further examples of doing things the hard way appear in a building full of farm implements. The ice-harvesting plow implies no rest for the weary farmer, even after he had hung up his corn binder and hay knives for the winter. The village would not, of course, be complete without a cheese factory, of which Green County had 200 a century ago.

Knowledgeable local guides conduct the tours and add interesting asides about their relatives. The Swiss Historical Village, 612 Seventh Avenue, is open daily 10:00 A.M. to 4:00 P.M. from May 1 through October 31. Admission charge. For more information call (608) 527–2317 or see www.swisshistorical village.com.

*The Tourist Troll is one of several
trolls from Scandinavian folklore along the Trollway
of downtown Mount Horeb. Michael J. Feeney is the artist.*

THE HILLS ARE ALIVE WITH THE SOUND OF ALPHORNS
New Glarus

New Glarus preserves its Swiss heritage with some unique traditions. For one thing, it has a yodel club, the only one in America, which is responsible for not only much of the yodeling that goes on at its festivals but also the alphorn blowing and the flag throwing.

It holds three annual festivals: the Heidi Festival in June, whose highlight is a play presented by local actors (and goats and kittens) about the little Swiss girl with braids and her gruff grandfather; Volksfest, which celebrates Swiss Independence Day on the first Sunday in August at Wilhelm Tell Schützenpark (that's shooting park); and the Wilhelm Tell Festival on Labor Day weekend, with outdoor performances by a large cast of local actors (and goats, cows, and horses) telling the Tell story, in English and German. In addition, all three festivals feature a lot of singing and yodeling and playing of accordions and alphorns. And flag throwing (though nobody remembers what flag throwing is about).

The man who gets credit for the town's first production of Friedrich Schiller's *Wilhelm Tell,* in 1938, is Edwin Barlow. A world traveler with childhood ties to New Glarus and a flair for the dramatic, he returned with visions of staging the drama and building a chalet. The drama has been repeated every year since then, and the chalet is now a museum with an amazing collection from Barlow's travels. Did he shop! Here, for example, are such one-of-a-kind items as Empress Carlotta's jewelry, King Louis XVI's watch, and chips from Pope Innocent III's skull, among three floors of other relics, woodcarvings, scissors cuttings, china, furniture, dolls, and artwork. Once

*Swiss herdsmen used alphorns to call home
before they had cell phones.*

Barlow's home, it is now Chalet of the Golden Fleece. Located at
618 Second Street, the museum is open from 10:00 A.M. to 4:00
P.M. Thursday through Monday, Memorial Day weekend
through October 31. Admission charge. For more information
call (608) 527–2614.

Of all this Swissness, one longtime resident observed that
New Glarus is more Swiss than Switzerland. For more see
www.swisstown.com or call (800) 527–6838.

Leon Varjian led the
Boom Box Parade around the capitol in Madison in 1983 to
the tune of "Stars and Stripes Forever," courtesy of station
WORT. The fifty band members wore red jackets; the mayor
wore a black tuxedo.

Look What I Found with the Dust Bunnies!

Oconomowoc

It's supposed to be good luck to find a cat whisker, so over the years Pauline Bemis got in the habit of picking up a whisker if she happened to see one lying there. She placed each one on a little shelf behind the glass door of a grandfather clock, and by now she has a large bundle of cat whiskers, hundreds of them.

The cats that she has owned over the past fifteen years are all represented in the collection: Little Caesar, Figaro, Zachary Robert, Pepper, Mitzie, Tiger, and Blackie. On average a cat probably has twenty-four whiskers, twelve on each side of the nose.

Pauline also has a large rock collection, which was featured at the Oconomowoc Public Library. Just for fun, she included the cat whiskers in the exhibit. Did people ask a lot of questions about the rocks? Not really. They were more curious about the cat whiskers.

Pauline has never counted them and has too many other things to do than sit around counting cat whiskers. Though semiretired, she teaches about woodwind instruments at two schools, gives private lessons, repairs instruments, and directs a hand-bell choir at church. In 1999 she received Oconomowoc's annual civic award in recognition of her musical involvement and other volunteer efforts.

S PEED S ITTING, I M EAN,
S EED S PITTING
Pardeeville

Various talents are useful at Pardeeville's Watermelon Festival. Those with oral gifts can enter the United States Watermelon-Eating and Seed-Spitting Championships. Those with artistic talents can enter the melon-sculpture contest. Spitting contestants select their seeds from the official

An aquarium of rare
watermelon fish at the festival in Pardeeville.

wedges, toe the starting line, and wind up, so to speak, as officials with measuring tapes scamper to record the distance. The record holder in the Men's Open spat his seed an amazing 61 feet 3 inches. Eating contestants sit at picnic tables, bury their heads in their watermelon wedges, and await the starting signal. The best record for eating is 2.98 seconds for one-eighth of a regulation-size melon.

No one has to compete to eat, and tons of watermelon are served free to all. First Saturday after Labor Day in Chandler Park, just north of the business district.

Return of the Two-Headed Pig
Poynette

The MacKenzie Environmental Center made headlines in May 1999 when the two-headed pig disappeared from its Aliens Museum. The pig was kept in a one-gallon jar filled with formaldehyde, displayed alongside some of nature's other curiosities. As a sign at the museum entrance gently explains to visiting schoolchildren, OCCASIONALLY IN NATURE ABNORMAL PLANTS AND ANIMALS OCCUR.

"Nothing is sacred," said the sheriff, and announced a $1,000 reward for information through the Crimestoppers tip line. Two farmers who each happened to have two-bodied, one-headed pigs in jars called to offer them to the museum. "It was real nice of them," said the sheriff. Finally, more than three weeks later, the pig was found on a hiking trail. Sheriff's deputies rushed it to Divine Savior Hospital in Portage to top off the formaldehyde and returned it to the museum. Today the pig is again in the display case that it shares with a four-legged pheasant and a Siamese raccoon.

Other exhibits at the Aliens Museum show a white wood-chuck, a white gray squirrel, a white white-tailed deer, a white flatheaded catfish, a white porcupine (examples of albinism); a black red fox, a black gray squirrel (melanism); and a one-antlered deer skull (hermaphroditism).

MacKenzie Environmental Education Center, W7303 County Highway CS, off Highway Q east of Poynette, occupies 280 acres and features wildlife exhibits, museums, and hiking trails. The grounds are open from dawn to dusk year-round except during deer gun season; wildlife exhibit and museums are open daily 8:00 A.M. to 4:00 P.M. May 1 to mid-October; 8:00 A.M. to 4:00 P.M. Monday through Friday in winter; closed on winter holidays. Call (608) 635–8110 for information.

THE CHICAGO TYPEWRITER
Racine

In the middle of the afternoon on November 20, 1933, John Dillinger and five henchmen entered American Trades Bank at Fifth and Main in downtown Racine and told everybody to reach for the sky. An exhibit in the lobby of the Racine Police Station tells what happened after that. Dillinger and his gang took $27,000—and, for their getaway, a policeman's .45-caliber Thompson machine gun and two human shields, the bank president and a bookkeeper.

The exhibit includes the Tommy gun, which was recovered later with *John Dillinger* etched into the stock, and elaborates on the gun's role in bootleggers' drive-by shootings and its vivid nickname, the "Chicago Typewriter." It also contains the black shoestrings that the gang used to tie the bank president and the bookkeeper to a tree somewhere in Waukesha County.

SMELT-O-RAMA

*I*f you're not from around here, you might find it odd to see grown men in snowmobile suits hanging over a bridge at night, lowering large nets on pulleys and shining flashlights into the water. But after you live here a while, you might not only think nothing of it, you might join them!

It's smelting! (Pronounced with a "sh-" for complete authenticity.) Don't let the fact that they're biting the heads off the live little fish put you off; that merely appeases the smelt gods to ensure a good harvest. The smelt start running to spawn in mid-April (at night, of course; no one likes to be seen spawning) in Lake Michigan and in inland lakes across Wisconsin. You've got to eat the tails, although the heads are optional, according to local custom. They come one way: battered, deep fried, and washed down with beer, although some folks like to slide 'em down with horseradish, hot sauce, tartar sauce, or, I know, beer. They're delicious, but you've got to eat a lot of them.

Curious? To give them a try, head for downtown Port Washington on the first weekend after Easter. The Van Ells–Schanern Post 82 American Legion (414–284–4690) typically feeds more than a ton of smelt to some 2,000 or 3,000 aficionados—it's a fund-raiser, so you can feel good about it. Bring your own coolers of beer, and butter and condiments, if needed. The smelt feast takes place at the Memorial Building in Lake Park, on the lakefront.

Whatever you do, remember the tails (or the tail patrol will get you), and don't even think of asking for the batter recipe—it's a secret. But odds are beer helps it cling.

Shoestrings? The exhibit says they were donated to the Kenosha County Historical Museum by the bookkeeper, Ursula Patzke.

Apparently Dillinger made the most of his few years on Earth. He stole forty-one chickens from Homer Zook at age twenty, spent nine years in prison for robbing an elderly grocer, and worked his way up to "Public Enemy Number One" before being gunned down at age thirty-one. His WANTED description and set of prints are here, too.

The Police Department is at 730 Center Street (Highway 32) in downtown Racine.

THE AVIS OF GROUNDHOGS
Sun Prairie

Jimmy the Groundhog lives on a small farm outside of Sun Prairie in a cement hutch with windows and a bed of hay. Once a year, early in the morning on February 2, a limousine pulls up outside Jimmy's little hutch and transports him into town. Television crews, reporters, city officials, and many others await his arrival. If Jimmy casts a shadow when he emerges from the limo, spring weather is more than six weeks away. The eight generations of Jimmys—like heirs to the throne, they're all related—claim better than 79 percent accuracy. After Jimmy has or has not cast a shadow, he goes on display and you can have your picture taken with him, like Santa Claus.

This Sun Prairie tradition of more than fifty years' standing is followed by breakfast and entertainment. It is preceded, on the Saturday before Groundhog Day, by the Groundhog Ball. Call (608) 837–4547 for details.

PRAIRIE-STYLE,
BUCKET INCLUDED

"*Wingspread,*" *a spectacular Frank Lloyd Wright house of the 1930s, has a fireplace with an opening tall enough for 12-foot logs to stand on end vertically. This innovative design proved impractical because logs burn from the bottom and eventually fall out into the room. Another inventive feature was the disappearing table. At the end of each course, the kitchen staff could pull the table into the kitchen, prepare it for the next course, and slide it back out to the dinner guests. Innovative furniture was also designed for Wright's Administration Building, next to the Research Tower shown on p. 174: three-legged office chairs that promoted good posture. Like some other Wright buildings, at first it had a leaky roof. Wright responded to complaints with "That's how you can tell it's a roof," "That's what happens when you leave a work of art out in the rain," and "Move your chair." The Johnson Foundation operates Wingspread as a conference facility. It is on Lighthouse Drive in Racine. Public tours are limited to Tuesday through Thursday, from 9:30 A.M. to 3:00 P.M. No tours are given during conferences. Check the conference schedule at www.johnsonfdn.org/upcoming.html, and then call (262) 681–3353.*

*A Frank Lloyd Wright–
designed white elephant, the Research Tower
at the S. C. Johnson headquarters in Racine. It has been
standing empty for about thirty years because it doesn't
meet safety codes.*

NOODLED UNTO DEATH
Watertown

Some years ago Watertown Goose was an impressive item on the menus of railroad dining cars and elegant restaurants in big cities. But how many fine lady and gentleman diners had a clue about what was going on in Watertown, Wisconsin?

Watertown geese were prized because they had been pampered, hand fed, and *over*fed until they were hugely overweight, by about twenty pounds. (The geese had correspondingly large livers, which translated into pâté de foie gras.) This was accomplished by force feeding them specially prepared noodles—big, fat multigrain noodles the size of sausages.

About four weeks before marketing time, a farmer schooled in the noodled-goose tradition began to make the rounds of his flock, holding each beak open with one hand and dropping the noodles down with the other. Each goose had to be fed several noodles every four or five hours around the clock. This meant that the entire family of a goose-noodler was involved, what with preparing special noodles (guess whose job that was?) and getting up at all hours of the night to noodle the geese.

Geese that got too fat to stand up anymore spent their last days in hammock contraptions. The largest Watertown goose ever shipped weighed 38½ pounds; the average was about 25. In one outstanding year 150,000 pounds of geese were shipped out of Watertown.

This famous local practice began in the 1880s and went on until twentieth-century federal meat-inspection laws forbade commercial butchering in the home—unless, of course, the goose-noodler's family hadn't already discovered that life had more to offer than this.

This stuffed overstuffed goose can be seen in the barn behind Octagon House in Watertown, along with pale-red models of livers of a noodled goose (on the right) and a normal goose (left).

But the geese that gave their lives for the greater glory of Watertown have not been forgotten. For one thing, the Watertown High School athletic teams are still called the Goslings. For another, thanks to taxidermy, you can see a noodled goose, accompanied by livers (both noodled and normal), in Plank Road Barn behind Octagon House.

Octagon House, a popular Watertown landmark, is an eight-sided, fifty-seven-room brick house that was completed in 1854 as a family residence. On the grounds is the building where Margarethe Meyer Schurz began the first kindergarten in the United States, in 1856. Its interior depicts a class in session and displays some early teaching tools.

The historic buildings on the property are open to the public daily from May 1 through October 31. Hours are 10:00 A.M. to 4:00 P.M. Memorial Day through Labor Day, 11:00 A.M. to 3:00 P.M. the rest of the time. Tours begin on the hour. Admission charge. For more information call (920) 261–2796.

*W*isconsin, birthplace of the blow dryer. Two companies that were developing electric blenders—Racine Universal Motor and Hamilton Beach of Two Rivers—were aware that women were using vacuum cleaners to dry their hair. They combined the technologies, and the first successful model was introduced in 1951. It had a nozzle attached to a pink plastic bonnet that fit over the head.

A WING AND A PRAYER
Waukesha

One fine morning in September 1941, flight instructor Dean Crites and his twenty-two-year-old student inspected their two-seater plane and took off from Milwaukee's Curtiss-Wright Airport (today Timmerman Field) for what was to be the student's graduation flight. They had just ascended to a thousand feet when suddenly there was a loud bang and a big jolt. The tail dropped, and the plane stalled and started in a loop. The student gladly turned the controls over to the instructor, who glided to a safe landing in an alfalfa field.

Not until they were on the ground did they discover that the entire engine had fallen out of the plane. (It was later pried out of Wisconsin Memorial Park cemetery, where it had been found buried a foot deep.) The very next day the brave lad went up again for his flight test.

A broken propeller blade on display at Waukesha County Airport represents all that is left of the plane today. Other exhibits tell the history of local aviation, from farm fields to jet landing strips. It began in 1912 with eighteen-year-old John Kaminski of Milwaukee, who performed exhibition flights in *Sweetheart*, a Curtiss Pusher biplane that had to be dismantled, shipped by train, and reassembled at the next air show. They

The principal product of Van Holten, Inc., of Waterloo is a pickle in a pouch. After dealing in vinegar, pickles, and sauerkraut for forty years, in 1939 the company invented the process of the individually packaged pickle. Today it is America's number-one producer of such a thing. People who need a quick pickle hit buy thousands of them at truck stops, movie theaters, convenience stores, concession stands, and prisons. For a total pickle experience, they tip the plastic pouch and drink the brine. More information and historic pictures of people packing pickles appear at www.vanholtenpickles.com.

tell more about Dean Crites, who could pick up a handkerchief with the wing tip of his WACO 10, and his brother Dale, pioneer aviators who built their first glider in 1919 and started the local flying school.

Mementos of simpler times include a pocket-size circle of plastic embossed with lines and numbers called a "Time-Speed Distance Computer," a slim pamphlet entitled *How to Fly a Piper Cub*, aviation helmets, and Dale Crites's tan flight suit.

The exhibits are housed in the spiffy new terminal of Waukesha County Airport/Crites Field, 2525 Aviation Drive. More information is available by calling (262) 521–5249 or visiting the Web site at www.critesfield.com. From exit 294 off I–94, go south on County Highway J for 1 mile, then travel west on Northview Road for ½ mile, then north on Aviation Drive to the terminal.

A CLAIM TO FAME
PREVIOUSLY OVERLOOKED
Waukesha

Dave Kremer is the greatest stacker of bowling balls in the world. His unique skill began about ten years ago at a bowling alley. Just for his own entertainment—because, he says, he is not much of a bowler of bowling balls—he balanced one bowling ball on top of another ball and then a third on top of those two. There they stood. An onlooker was impressed. "Do it again and I'll pay you," he said, and became Dave's agent.

After practicing for several years in his garage in Waukesha, Dave earned a place in the bizarre-skills category of the *Guinness Book of World Records*—probably a permanent place, since he seems also to be the world's *only* bowling-ball stacker. His record is eleven balls. A challenger would need steady

Dave Kremer has to practice in the garage.

hands, good eyes, sturdy toes, a sense of humor, luck, an indulgent mate if any, and an appreciation for bowling-ball shape (bowling balls aren't perfectly round) and weight distribution.

Dave Kremer has a real job and a wife and four young boys, and he doesn't stack bowling balls every day. But stacking them for fun has led to trips all over the world and to appearances on such TV shows as *Live with Regis and Kathie Lee* (Kathie kissed him on the head) and *Ripley's Believe It or Not*. He was also the December page in Guinness's year 2000 calendar.

WHERE THE WILDERNESS
MEETS CONGO BONGO
Wisconsin Dells

Where to begin? The Dells—the Midwest's most popular family vacation spot, one of America's most amazing tourism meccas—offers an embarrassment of riches.

Warming up at Tommy Bartlett's
Thrill Show. What next? The incredible trapeze toe-hang?

There's Air Boingo Bungee Jump, Extreme World, Count Wolff Von Baldasar's Haunted Mansion, and Mass Panic. Noah's Ark, America's largest indoor water park, has three miles of waterslides, 5,000 inner tubes, and such options for getting wet as Congo Bongo Rapids, Kowabunga, and Flash Flood.

With places like Serpent Safari, Laser Storm, and about eighty other major attractions to choose from, it's no wonder many people who come to the Dells stay for days without ever seeing the dells—the part that began millions of years BTB (Before Tommy Bartlett). In relative peace and quiet, guides on boat tours point out unique rock formations along the beautiful Wisconsin River: Cow in the Milk Bottle, Devil's Elbow, Baby Grand Piano, Hawk's Bill. Some of the boats are ducks, modified World War II amphibious vehicles.

The name "Tommy Bartlett" means waterskiing, bumper stickers, and the presence of a Russian MIR space station at the Dells. In the 1950s Bartlett started the Thrill Show on Water, which inspired other spectacles and remains a classic. The Dells wasn't just for fishing anymore.

The Dells occupies about 20 square miles of the communities of Wisconsin Dells and Lake Delton to the east of I–90/94. Outdoor attractions are open Memorial Day through Labor Day. Many indoor attractions are open year-round. All charge admission. Details at www.wisdells.com.

THE WONDER SPOT
Wisconsin Dells

The gravity-defying Wonder Spot is in a class by itself, and not only because it's located in a pretty wooded setting just off the main drag. Water flows upward, chairs balance on two legs, people lean at weird angles. Everything is a bit off kilter, as it has been since someone built a cabin here in 1948 and abandoned it because he said a mysterious force made him unable to walk, pour, or see straight when he lived here. Visitors agree it's a goofy place.

Take Highway 12 South, turn right at Sarento's Restaurant, and follow the road around back to the Wonder Spot. Open daily 9:00 A.M. to 9:00 P.M. in the summer. Admission charge. Call (608) 254–4224 for more information.

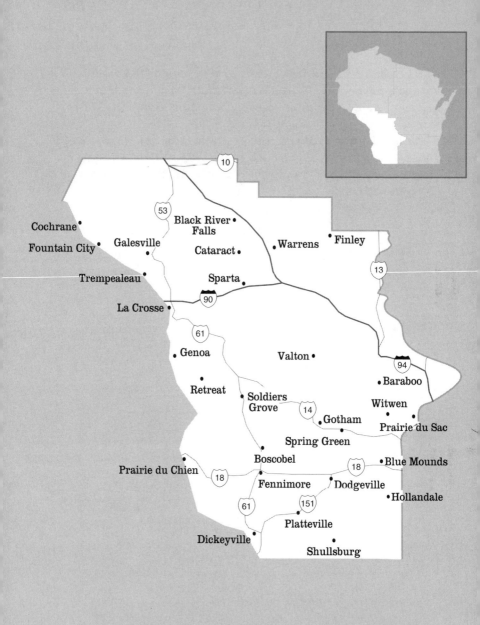

Cochrane

Fountain City

Galesville

Black River
Falls

Cataract

Warrens

Finley

Trempealeau

Sparta

La Crosse

Genoa

Valton

Baraboo

Retreat

Soldiers
Grove

Gotham

Witwen

Prairie du Sac

Spring Green

Boscobel

Blue Mounds

Prairie du Chien

Fennimore

Dodgeville

Hollandale

Platteville

Dickeyville

Shullsburg

10

53

13

90

61

94

14

18

18

61

151

SOUTHWEST

SOUTHWEST

Wisconsin's west coast: Instead of the Pacific Ocean, the Mississippi River. Instead of Malibu or Carmel or San Francisco, think Cassville or La Crosse or Buffalo City. Instead of some thousand-dollar-a-night beach house, try a B&B overlooking the Mississippi. One of them has a National Register of Historic Places sign in front and the following notice inside: "If no one is here, go upstairs and pick a room, keys are in the door. Leave a check [$30] on the dresser. Welcome." These river towns hold many such charms.

Inland, the southwest section of Wisconsin is rich in the works of visionary artists, self-taught locals with the urge to say something patriotic, something religious, something personal, something off-the-wall. Years ago they said it with cement, creating massive folk sculptures and smashing the family crockery (that must have been cathartic) for embellishments. Sometimes, a visit to the Dickeyville Grotto was all it took to unleash the artist within. Today, outsider artists are more likely to work in the medium of industrial debris, possibly inspired by the genius of Dr. Evermor's Art Park, south of Baraboo.

In this southwest section of *Wisconsin Curiosities* you will not learn how the town of Eleva got its name. According to a popular version of its derivation, the man who was hired to paint the word *elevator* on a grain elevator quit before painting the last three letters. People coming through the area assumed that Eleva was the name of the town and it stuck. Nitpicky historians, however, disagree, and their less-entertaining versions made it no fun to even bring up the subject.

But there are lots of other things to tell about this part of Wisconsin.

SOMETHING OUT OF NOTHING
Baraboo

Several metal creatures alongside the highway and a simple DELANEY'S SURPLUS sign identify Dr. Evermor's location, but they hardly prepare you for what lies behind the trees and down the driveway. It's a fantastic garden of scrap metal, now assembled into giant insectoids and birds; a philharmonic-size bird orchestra; and the 400-ton Forevertron, the world's largest scrap-metal sculpture, according to the *Guinness Book of World Records*.

Early in the 1940s, when he was little Tom Every growing up in Brooklyn, Wisconsin, Dr. Evermor was flattening tin cans and toothpaste tubes and saving foil from gum wrappers for the war effort, along with everyone else. With this early conditioning in recycling, he grew up to run an industrial salvage business and to appreciate what industrial designers could do with iron, steel, brass, bronze, and copper. He also developed a fine collection of dynamos, survey markers, sheet metal, springs, pipes, chains, chimes, wrenches, musical instruments, blades, cables, the decontamination chamber from the Apollo space mission, and much, much more. With these materials he creates gigantic yet intricate sculptures.

The Forevertron represents Dr. Evermor's plan to travel to the heavens, as a scientist or professor of 1890 might have imagined doing inside a copper egg propelled by a magnetic lightning-force beam. Nearly everything else here is centered on the idea—the Celestial Listening Ears, the Graviton, the Juicer Bug, even the Bird Band, which will be playing as Dr. Evermor sails away. Visiting engineers appreciate the fact that its components are salvage from late-nineteenth-century factories.

Dr. Evermor's Forevertron,
the world's largest scrap-metal sculpture.

Dr. Evermor is a self-taught artist who uses no blueprints, no sketches, nothing. He doesn't even think about it—"I just go for it." His work attracts television crews, filmmakers, artists, inventors, children, and a great assortment of humanity.

Dr. Evermor's Art Park is on the west side of Highway 12, just north of County Highway C, and 7 miles south of the Baraboo city limits. Consistent with the creator's spirit, there are no tours, no admission fee, no signs to explain anything. But there might be Dr. Evermor—he's often on-site—in pith helmet with cigar.

FLAP YOUR ELBOWS, SPIN YOUR EARS, AND FLY AWAY
Baraboo

The International Crane Foundation has every species of crane in the world—and George Archibald. He too is a tall and rare bird. "I'd do almost anything for a crane!" says Archibald, director of ICF.

Archibald's earliest childhood memory is of being two years old and crawling after a mother duck and her ducklings. When he got older his parents let him raise chickens, ducks, pheasants, turkeys, and even peacocks. By the time he was out of college, he was dancing around like a crane to encourage female cranes to lay eggs and dressing up like a crane to take care of young birds.

It's all very scientific, as he has explained to audiences far and wide; a newborn crane thinks that the first large moving thing it sees is its mother, so it's important to establish the crane image from the start. Endangered cranes all over the world were in big trouble before Archibald and others at ICF came to their rescue, and they're all breathing easier now.

The International Crane Foundation is the only place in the world where you can see all fifteen of the world's crane species, including the sarus crane, at 6 feet easily the tallest flying bird in the world. You might also see some staff "chick parents" dressed like cranes. From chick parents baby cranes learn where to find food, how to go to water, and to be alert.

ICF is about 5 miles north of Baraboo and 1 mile east of Highway 12 on Shady Lane Road. Hours are from 9:00 A.M. to 5:00 P.M. daily, April 15 through October 31. Admission charge. For information about cranes, special events, and tours, see the ICF's Web site at www.savingcranes.org or call (608) 356–9462.

A chick parent at the International Crane Foundation wears a crane costume so that the birds don't get too attached to humans.

CIRCUS WORLD MUSEUM
Baraboo

Baraboo is the only place in Wisconsin where elephants splash in the river in summertime. They're taking a break before it's back to work at the Big Top Show at the Circus World Museum.

The year-round exhibit hall has such novel sights as the sparkly little wedding clothes of "the smallest man in the world," 33-inch Michu, and his bride, Julianna, also a little person but several inches taller. Though never husband and wife, they recited marriage vows twice a day throughout 1976 and 1977 in mock ceremonies before thousands of witnesses, reenacting the storied wedding of Tom Thumb and his bride in 1863. The chair that Clyde Beatty used in his wild-animal act is here, too. It's an ordinary kitchen chair with one leg missing (gnawed off?). You can also learn about the canvas tutus worn by elephants that performed in an original Balanchine-Stravinsky ballet and about the night in 1885 when a speeding train plowed into Jumbo the elephant. Posters tell of intrepid, intricate feats on a single strand of wire at dizzying heights.

It's all here because Baraboo was home until about 1918 to the Ringling Brothers, "The World's Greatest Showmen" (they started out with a small tent, three horses, and a hyena), and to their circus as well.

Located at 550 Water Street (Highway 113). Circus performances daily from early May through Labor Day. Exhibit hall, circus-wagon pavilion, and wagon-restoration center open daily year-round except major holidays. Admission charge. Toll-free number is (866) 693–1500, or see www.circusworld museum.com.

WISCONSIN DEATH TRAP
Black River Falls

In an ordinary winter, Black River Falls is an outdoor paradise for snowmobilers, cross-country skiers, dogsledders, and snowboarders. Once it warms, the Black River and the state forest surrounding the handsome little community provide virtually every kind of outdoor experience you could hope for. As the chamber of commerce likes to say, "Nowhere in this great continent of ours can be found a more desirable residence."

It's just that, for a few years back in the 1890s, everyone in Black River Falls seemed to go crazy. Michael Lesy captured it in his book *Wisconsin Death Trip* (1973), a pastiche of mortuary photographs, newspaper clippings, and admissions records of the Mendota Mental Asylum culled from the *Badger State Banner*, a tabloid published in Black River Falls by Frank and George Cooper that leaned heavily toward human interest and misery.

For whatever reasons—economic or personal depression, disease, crop failure, just plain loneliness (some have even cited "ethnic tendencies of the Scandinavian and German populations")—all manner of weird goings-on went on. Windows were smashed, children ran wild, fires were set, farmers used dynamite for pillows, and chickens were decapitated in bizarre rituals, all recorded by photographer Charles Van Schaick, whose studios now house the Jackson County Historical Society (where the number-one attraction is his "Wisconsin Death Trip" collection).

It could be that this sort of thing went on in isolated rural areas everywhere in the Midwest, but there was just no Van Schaick to record it. *Wisconsin Death Trip* is now a cottage industry in Black River Falls, and the 1999 film of the same name by James Marsh has stirred the pot. The original photos are housed at the Van Schaick Photo Gallery, 13 South First Street, where researchers may view them by appointment. Call (715) 284-5314. In the near future the Jackson County Historical Society plans to open a photo gallery of his work at its museum at 321 Main Street. Hours are 11:00 A.M. to 3:00 P.M. Friday and Saturday, Memorial Day to Labor Day.

THOU SHALT NOT
STEAL THE TOILETRIES
Boscobel

Janesville salesman John "Nick" Nicholson had had a hard
day on the road when he checked in to the Boscobel Hotel,
or "Central House," as it was known in 1898. He was not
pleased (1) to learn that no single rooms were available, and
(2) to find the hotel "crowded with drummers and hang-abouts
playing cards, shaking dice, smoking, laughing, cursing,
yelling and singing with clinking of glasses and men drunk
and asleep in chairs." He was, however, willing to share a double room (Room 19) with, as it turned out, a kindred spirit,
Beloit salesman Sam Hill.

Nicholson and Hill agreed that "Christian traveling men"
needed suitable ways to pass the time, so they organized what
eventually became the Gideons International Society. Today the
Gideons make sure that hotel rooms all over the world contain
Bibles—that's about 59 million Bibles per year, or 112 night-
stand drawers per minute.

Senator John F. Kennedy and his wife, Jacqueline, occupied
Room 19 for a few hours on the afternoon of March 25, 1960,
and then had dinner. JFK was campaigning for the Democratic
nomination for president, and the Wisconsin primary was coming up. It is not known how much of that time they spent on
Bible study.

The local historical society has outfitted Room 19 in period
furniture, and you can ask to see it by calling (608) 375–4714.
The 1863 building isn't functioning as a hotel now, but it has a
restaurant and bar (closed on Sunday), as well as a lobby that
displays Gideon Bibles in several languages. It is located on
Wisconsin Avenue in downtown Boscobel.

This 12-foot fiberglass mouse is named for the great Russian composer Igor Stravinsky, who died on the day that Igor arrived in Fennimore, April 6, 1971. He stands in front of Fennimore Cheese on Highway 61 on the south side of Fennimore.

AND ON THE SEVENTH DAY
THE WEGNERS RESTED
Cataract

*B*efore the era of television and professional football, families piled into the car and went out for Sunday drives. In this part of Wisconsin, one of the places they headed for, if not over, was Cataract.

The big attraction was the concrete-and-glass creations of Paul and Matilda Wegner. Cars lined up for miles to see the church, the steamship, the anniversary cake, an American flag—thirty sculptures in all. A peace monument even became a "speakers' corner" for preachers and politicians.

The Wegners created all of this during their retirement. They were German immigrants who first farmed and later ran the Ford dealership in the nearby town of Bangor. (They raised five children along the way.) Then one day in 1929, they ventured south to Dickeyville and beheld Father Wernerus's grotto (page 199). After that experience, sculptures and structures with themes of patriotism, religion, and travel began taking shape on their own property.

The Wegners used pieces of glass and pottery, many a blue transformer, here and there a doorknob, and, of course, concrete. The profusely embellished exterior of the glass church has views of eleven different churches; the interior is equally intricate. It was the scene of many weddings as well as Paul Wegner's funeral. The steamship represents the Wegners' voyage to this country in 1886, and the giant wedding cake honors their fifty-two years together.

The Wegners embellished their steamship with seashells,
plumbing pipes, and drainage pipes.

The Kohler Foundation funded restoration of the site and
deeded the Paul and Matilda Wegner Grotto to Monroe County,
which maintains it as an outdoor museum and public park.
Located on Highway 71, 9%0 miles north of Sparta or 1½ miles
south of Cataract, it is open year-round. For information call
the Monroe County Local History Room at (608) 269–8680.

Hazards off the bike trail: at the corner of Highway M and Fitchburg Road south of Fitchburg (top) and between Highway ID and South Street in Blue Mounds (bottom).

ONE CURE FOR OLD-AGE BOREDOM
Cochrane

Herman Rusch was another energetic, self-taught, late-blooming artist who emerged in the 1950s. At age seventy-one he discovered his medium to be glass and cement. He proceeded to spread his whimsical dinosaurs, flamingos, polar bears, snakes, and a Hindu temple over several acres of land south of Cochrane, near the Mississippi River. He also surrounded them with ornamental spires and gates and enclosed them in a spectacular, 260-foot-long arching fence. "You could go around the world five times and never see another like it," he said.

Herman Rusch's signature piece.

Rusch's work has won high praise for its sense of design and wit, but Herman seemed not to have taken himself too seriously. According to the inscription on a bust of himself, creating this wondrous world was just "a good way to kill old-age boredom." He died in 1985, eleven days after his one hundredth birthday, having successfully lived up to his claim that "a fellow should leave a few tracks."

Herman's "tracks" were restored by the Kohler Foundation, which also assisted with the addition of a new exhibit, a collection of eighteen miniature buildings modeled after actual buildings in Cochrane. About 2 feet tall, they were created in the Depression era by yet another self-taught artist, Fred Schlosstein, in his backyard on Main Street and now stand in the Prairie Moon museum. To reach Prairie Moon Sculpture Garden and Museum, take Highway 35 northwest from Fountain City about 6 miles. Just past the Cochrane–Fountain City School, turn left onto Prairie Moon Road; the site is located half a mile farther, on the left. The garden is open year-round, dawn to dusk. The museum is open 1:00 to 4:00 P.M. Saturday from Memorial Day to Labor Day or by appointment. Call (608) 687–8250 for more information.

HOLY GHOST PARK
Dickeyville

In both mass and message, the Dickeyville Grotto is the weightiest of Wisconsin's cement parks. No whimsical creatures cavort here. Instead there are awesome altars and shrines labeled with straightforward commands—FAITH, PEACE, CHASTITY, MILDNESS, LONG SUFFERING, PATIENCE, FORTITUDE—and encrusted with glassware, pottery, fossils, Indian relics, and hornets' nests.

One of the "Religion in Stone" areas at Holy Ghost Park at Dickeyville.

This is the work of Father Mathias Wernerus, who, in the 1920s, saw it as "God's wonderful material collected from all parts of the world . . . Future generations will still enjoy the fruit of our labor and will bless the man that conceived and built this thing." He was right. Each year about 60,000 people view the altars, shrines, fountains, gardens, and sculptures on the grounds of Holy Ghost Parish.

Father Wernerus, a missionary priest who grew up among outdoor shrines in Germany, had a lot of assistance from parishioners and schoolchildren. They hauled rocks and concrete, contributed materials from home, and helped with decoration and construction. The Dickeyville Grotto is actually a collaborative project representing the geology of the upper Mississippi region, the religious and patriotic beliefs of Father Wernerus and his parishioners, and the crockery and figurines of their combined households.

The grotto is on Highway 61 just north of Dickeyville. Grounds open year-round. Tours daily in summer months. Gift shop open daily from April through October, then weekends until Christmas. Call (608) 568–3119 for details.

IS THAT A STRATOCRUISER OR ARE YOU JUST HAPPY TO SEE ME?
Dodgeville

A few miles south of House on the Rock (p. 226), while your head is still spinning, you come upon a Boeing C-97 Stratocruiser parked alongside Highway 23. It's the size of half a football field, and during the Korean War it transported troops and cargo.

It's a landmark for the Don Q Inn, which lies just beyond. The elaborate plans that Don Quinn, who owned the hotel then, had in mind for the plane didn't quite work out, but other ideas have. The Dodgeville train station was moved here and converted to sleeping rooms, the steeple from an 1850s Methodist church became a honeymoon suite, copper cheese vats were converted to bathtubs, and barber chairs from shops in Fennimore and an Iowa penitentiary offer seating in the lobby.

It isn't exactly the plane and local history that bring many people here, however. The Don Q has fantasy suites that offer travelers an opportunity to bed down in an igloo, a space capsule, a thatched jungle hut, and a hot-air balloon, among other novel accommodations.

The Whad'Ya Gnome hopes to meet a cute lit-
tle girl gnome at the Don Q tonight.

All this is connected to the Don Q restaurant by a damp, 300-foot-long stone tunnel. Highway 23 North. Call (608) 935–2321 for information.

COGITO, ERGO ZOOM
Finley

Did a few of the Cub Scouts seem bored on the tour of the cranberry bog? Were they dragging their feet on the nature trail? If so, here's a field trip that could be a winner: bombing practice at the Hardwood Range.

Here crews from Truax Field in Madison and other Midwest bases of the Air National Guard are training in their F-16s, F-15Es, and other incredibly fast planes. The bombs are inert, shadows of their former shells; no actual bombs are harmed in the preparation of these crews for combat. The targets vary: an old beat-up SCUD missile launcher, little bridges, fuel storage tanks, big orange bull's-eyes, jeeps, a rusty PT boat.

The range is more than 2 miles wide by 6 miles long, which is plenty of room for an F-16 to come screaming across the sky. You have to supply your own KABLAAAMs and BARROOOOOOMs, however, because the bombs don't make a sound; they just kick up a big gray cloud on the ground. The surrounding area is heavily wooded and probably devoid of forest creatures, who may have packed up and moved to the Necedah Wildlife Refuge on the other side of Highway 80. Flights are restricted there.

The public is welcome. Picnic tables, a Pepsi machine, a rest room, airplane posters for your bedroom wall, and earplugs are provided. From Necedah, go north on Highway 80 for about 12 miles to Highway F at Finley; turn right, follow Highway F for about 1 mile, and turn left at the Hardwood Range sign at Eleventh Avenue. Operates five or six days a week year-round. For a recorded message of the daily schedule, call (608) 427–1509. Read more about it at www.volkfield.ang.af.mil/Hardwood.htm.

A lot of people like cranberry bogs, but they're not for everyone.

HOUSE ON THE ROCK?
NO, ROCK IN THE HOUSE
Fountain City

At 11:38 A.M. on April 24, 1995, Maxine Anderson was admiring her newly decorated bedroom—the wallpaper with its tiny blue flowers and border of cabbage roses, the full-length mirrors on the closet doors—when she heard a noise that was worse than thunder. She headed for the door, and seconds later a fifty-five-ton boulder landed where she had been standing. For thousands of years it had hovered high up on the bluff behind the house. (Today you can look up and see the gap, like a missing tooth, in a row of boulders like this one.) The Andersons promptly moved out and sold the house as is, rock, debris, and all, to people with an eye for its tourism possibilities.

This is not the look the Andersons had in mind for the master bedroom.

Strangely enough, the same thing happened to a house next door in April 1901. This runaway rock, however, killed a Mrs. Dubler as she slept. Her husband awoke to find himself in the cellar amid the ruins of their home. A garage stands on the site now. Stranger still, yet another boulder—enormous, 200 tons—careened down the bluff in 2002, but only trees were in the way of that one.

Fountain City has antiques stores, art galleries, and a fatalistic population. Rock in the House is located toward the north end of town and faces the Mississippi River, at 440 North Shore Drive (Highway 35, the Great River Road). Open—is it ever—daily from 10:00 A.M. to 6:00 P.M., year-round.

THE JOY OF TOYS
Fountain City

*E*lmer Duellman owned forty cars by the time he was eighteen years old. It was a sign of things to come. Now in his fifties (and driving a red Nissan pickup truck), he shows what he's collected since then at Elmer's Auto and Toy Museum. Actually, Elmer likes anything with wheels. In addition to cars for grown-ups, he has more than 600 pedal cars—the Junior G-man cruiser with tommy gun mounted on the fender is especially eye-catching—and more than 100 pedal tractors. He even has a bookmobile.

Elmer's wheels and toys are housed in five positively jam-packed barnlike buildings. In one you can see everything from a two-tone green 1933 Rolls-Royce and a silver Corvette with 4½ miles on the odometer to a Gene Autry bike with fringed saddle bags bearing the Autry-twirling-his-lariat motif. Elsewhere behold an orange and black 1975 Excalibur Phaeton,

a 1968 Chevrolet Caprice, a 1929 Model A Ford Phaeton
(this last in the family room—Elmer is lucky that his wife,
Bernadette, shares his enthusiasm). Altogether they have more
than one hundred cars, plus great numbers of motorcycles,
scooters, riding toys, and antique toys and dolls.

To top it off, Elmer's Auto and Toy Museum has a
spectacular location on Eagle's Bluff, the highest point on the
Mississippi River, with a panoramic view of the main channel
and backwaters. To get there, take Highway 95 for half a mile
from Fountain City to Highway G, then go a quarter mile to
W903 Elmers Road. Admission charge. The hours are tricky—
something like every other weekend in summer—so before you
go, call (608) 687–7221.

S E R E N D I P I T Y   I N   H A R D W A R E
G e n o a

The words "Ohmigosh, I've been looking for this for years"
ring out at Old Tool Shed Antiques. Gayhart Swenson and
his son Rick lovingly rescue, clean, repair, display, and sell old
hand tools. Handmade tools are especially admired here, from
the simple plumb bobs that boys made in high school shop
class to very complex contraptions. In addition to hundreds of
hammers, chisels, and drills are the more offbeat fire-hose noz-
zles (Gay and Rick are both retired firefighters), rope winders,
ornate cast-iron tractor seats, goose-wing axes, denture makers, cigar-box openers, and much more that you'll never see at
Home Depot.

Some items at Old Tool Shed Antiques are so old that hardly
anyone knows what they ever were used for. *Hardly* anyone,
because it's really a matter of waiting for the right person to
come through the door. Not long ago a mystery tool sat on the

front counter for several months until at last a stranger entered the shop and with one glance announced, "I know what that is, and I have the instruction booklet at home." On his next visit, instructions and Mend-a-Rip (a hand-sewing device that cowboys carried to repair saddles and chaps) were reunited.

You might want to celebrate finding that wrench that completes your set over a platter of catfish cheeks at one of the local restaurants. Genoa (pronounced "GeNOa," despite its Italian heritage) is on the Mississippi River, 17 miles south of La Crosse on Highway 35 (the Great River Road). Old Tool Shed Antiques occupies an 1867 building at 612 Main Street. Open 10:00 A.M. to 5:00 P.M. Thursday through Monday, or by chance or appointment. Call (608) 689–2066.

E AT Y OUR H EART O UT ,
C LAES O LDENBURG
G o t h a m

In February 1999 a winter ice storm damaged a tall conifer in a small grove of Norwegian spruces at the Merry Farm of Gotham. When the broken branches were cleared away, the owners saw that the forces of Nature had selected their property as the site of a modern icon: a felt-tip marker, 9 feet tall. They commissioned a wood sculptor to smooth out the contours and added a bronze plaque declaring it a historical marker.

The marker stands between a brown house and a brown barn in a small grove of tall pine trees. The owners are friendly. The property has beautiful gardens and has been the scene of weddings (instead of saying "I will," one bride said, "If you change your attitude, I will"), barn dances, and folk concerts. Take Highway 14 to Gotham; go east on County High-

The historical felt-tip marker at
Merry Farm of Gotham, sculpture by Michael Feeney.

way JJ for three-quarters of a mile and north on Moss Hollow
for 1 mile; at the sharp turn right, go straight to the end of
Slow Lane to number 30999.

ART FOR NICK'S SAKE
Hollandale

Nicholas Engelbert was different from other dairy farmers. He read a book while walking his cows along the highway to graze (he owned only fourteen acres). And on the lawn of his farmhouse were all these creations that he put together when he got home: Paul Bunyan, Uncle Sam, Snow White and the Seven Dwarfs, Vikings, lions, elephants, eagles, peacocks. He used metal parts from around the barnyard, stones from the stream, glass and china from the kitchen, and concrete for glue. As if Nick had a lot of

Nick Engelbert depicted his family in this family tree. He and his wife are on the lower branches, their children are playing and doing hobbies they liked, and the fellow at the bottom is one of the tramps who enjoyed the Engelberts' hospitality over the years.

glass-and-concrete batter left over one day, the exterior of his
two-story house acquired a façade to match the sculpture.

The Engelbert place eventually became quite a roadside
attraction, so Nick provided a parking lot and picnic grounds
for visitors. Every year his wife planted flowers that spelled
out PEACE.

But Nick died on his eighty-first birthday in 1962, and his
artwork fell into disrepair. Pieces disappeared, though the
mailman tried to keep an eye on things. In 1991 the Kohler
Foundation came to the rescue. It restored many pieces, gave
Nick's place a name—Grandview—and turned the project over
to the Pecatonica Foundation, which operates Grandview as a
historic folk-art site. The house is open, and Nick's paintings of
family life hang on the walls.

Grandview is located on the south side of Highway 39 just
west of Hollandale. The house is open daily 10:00 A.M. to 4:00
P.M. from Memorial Day through Labor Day, on weekends only
in May and October, or at other times by appointment; the
grounds are open daily year-round. Call (608) 967–2151 or see
www.nicksgrandview.org for more information.

P O P - B O T T L E   G A R D E N
L a   C r o s s e

Paul Hefti's primary media are stuffed animals and green
plastic soft-drink bottles (if he needs red or white, he'll saw
off the bottom, paint the insides, and reassemble). His accent
pieces are ice-cream cartons, lamp bases, toys, plastic flowers,
and fans. His creations fill a large fenced-in corner lot, about
60 by 90 feet. Some are anchored to the ground, and some
hang from trees.

Holiday greetings from Paul Hefti, 1999.

Some are complex Rube Goldberg–style arrangements of bottles and tubes. Some are simple: A pale-yellow plastic locomotive perches on a pole to which a small bald doll is pinned by her hula hoop. A frilly lampshade tops off a plastic wishing well.

Alongside the house are small special-event shrines where bottles observe the season or spell out HAPPY BIRTHDAY TO YOU. A display called "It's Okay" consists of swags of green plastic bottles, a pink plastic dollhouse, a balding doll in a shredded gray dress, and stuffed animals whose identities have been lost to the elements. For Paul Hefti, who is in his eighties and lives in the small redbrick house, it's all a work in progress.

The world's largest six-pack is 54 feet high and holds 68,200 gallons of beer (enough to fill 1,223,466 normal six-packs) during the aging process. It is located at City Brewery just south of downtown La Crosse. Heading south on Rose Street (Highway 53), go 5 blocks past the blue bridge (Cass Street) and under the overpass to the six-pack and the City Brewery hospitality center.

Paul puts a lot of thought into his work, and although no single theme comes through, the overall effect is colorful and upbeat. Despite the severe La Crosse winters that they must endure, the large population of somewhat-the-worse-for-wear pandas, bunnies, bears, reindeer, and duckies constantly smile back at visitors to this jolly environment.

It is located at Fifth Avenue and Adams, just east of the curve in Highway 14 as it heads toward downtown La Crosse.

VALLEY OF THE DOLLS
La Crosse

If there's a doll in your past, no matter when, look here long enough and you're sure to see a familiar face. How could anyone be missing? The La Crosse Doll Museum has about 7,200 dolls on display, from early bisque to Jesse Ventura.

In addition to the mainstream favorites, there are child-star dolls (such as Deanna Durbin, Shirley Temple, and Buffy), advertising dolls (icons of Oscar Mayer, Tidy Cat, Morton Salt, Bubble Yum); and public figures (JFK and Jackie, Margaret Thatcher, and Abe Lincoln). There are baby dolls (one resembles Humphrey Bogart—he did, after all, pose for Gerber baby-food labels) and "less than pretty" dolls (including an Amy that escaped Rosalynn Carter's bonfire on the White House lawn). And if you think your Crissy With Hair That Grows and Grows and Grows was a first, a 1920s doll with a lever that moves her horse hair up and down shows that Crissy was not.

A display case 82 feet long contains the largest collection of Barbies in the Northern Hemisphere and in action. Barbie makes toast in her dream kitchen, she steps out with Dance Magic Ken, she paddles past her beach house. Each Barbie is displayed with her original outfits and accessories, in case you no longer remember the earrings that got lost the first day or the rightful owner of the white go-go boots.

Darlene Mueller, collector and curator, knows stories behind them all, and she sometimes dresses like Raggedy Ann for group tours. Her museum at 1213 Caledonia Street, in Old Towne North, is open 10:00 A.M. to 5:00 P.M. Monday through Saturday, 11:00 A.M. to 4:30 P.M. Sunday. Admission charge. Call (608) 785–0020 for more details.

ONE *BIG M*
Platteville

The 241-foot letter *M* that overlooks Grant County from a mound east of Platteville is the work of energetic and competitive students of the Wisconsin Mining School, circa the late 1930s. Other mining schools had big *M*'s, but the Wisconsin boys made sure that they hauled enough limestone to make their school's the biggest.

The *M* is lighted at night on two annual occasions: University of Wisconsin–Platteville homecoming in the fall, and the "M" Ball in the spring. Members of a coed professional engineering fraternity accomplish this by placing about 500 coffee cans around the outside of the *M*. Inside each can is a smaller can, with a few rocks between the two for ballast. Kerosene and a particle-board wick go into each smaller can. Theta Taus dash around with road flares lighting the wicks, and the *M* burns for about forty-five minutes.

In 1998 a member of the Platteville Jaycees had a brilliant idea. He rounded up about 250 Plattevillians who were willing to dress in black (black trash bags, if necessary), trudge up the 260 steps, and arrange themselves in the shape of mouse ears in the V part of the *M*. An aerial photographer snapped the

More than 260 steps lead to the top of the big M, but once there you'd have to be about 20 feet tall to view the world's largest W. You can, however, survey the countryside for miles around or zoom in on tiny cows with the telescope provided here (free—no quarters necessary).

scene, and the photo won for Platteville the grand prize in a nationwide contest sponsored by Disney: Mickey's Hometown Parade. On July Fourth about 50,000 people (many in mouse ears) lined Main Street to see such sights as thirty Disney floats; the Cuba City High School band in Pluto hats; and Mickey, Minnie, and Donald, waving and bowing. That night $100,000 worth of fireworks went off at the world's biggest *M*.

The *M* is about 4 miles northeast of Platteville on County Highway B, but it's best viewed from miles away. Students from the College of Engineering, Mathematics and Science maintain the *M*.

THE BEAUMONT DIET
Prairie du Chien

The exhibits on early medicine at the Prairie du Chien Museum at Fort Crawford are enough to make you shudder. Especially "Doctors on Horseback" from the 1840s. You'd have to be in pretty bad shape to be glad to see one of these guys coming up the driveway. In his saddlebags might be a pocket surgical kit of handmade instruments, a lancet or "scarificator" for bleed-

A diorama at the Fort Crawford medical museum depicts an amputation on a patient who appears to have passed out. Anesthesia didn't come along until 1846. Medicine was more casual then—doctors in street clothes, leg in bucket, surgical saw on floor.

ing, a turnkey for extracting teeth. But the price was right. In 1846 the bill for one patient came to only $46, including $10 for "amputating all the toes of one foot." Doc's snowshoes and lantern complete the picture in this exhibit.

Apparently things improved slightly later on. There were dentists with offices (and foot-operated drills) and horse-and-buggy doctors with manufactured, though still scary-looking, instruments that came in nice lined cases.

It was at Fort Crawford that Dr. William Beaumont conducted experiments on the hapless Alexis St. Martin, a voyageur who had suffered a gunshot wound to his left side that left a hole after it healed. Dr. Beaumont found it absolutely fascinating to tie bits of food to a string, drop them into the hole, then pull them out to see the effect of Alexis's stomach juices. This went on for several years of codependence, after which, in 1833, Dr. Beaumont published the book that explained the physiology of digestion once and for all. His work is recognized here, along with other milestones in medicine. Dioramas show foot-tall medical professionals calmly removing tumors and amputating limbs, the patients' little faces contorted in agony, until, at last, *anesthesia!* in 1846.

The Prairie du Chien Museum at Fort Crawford, 717 South Beaumont Road, is open daily 10:00 A.M. to 5:00 P.M. in June, July, and August, and to 4:00 P.M. in May, September, and October. Admission charge. Call (608) 326–6960 for more information.

REAL TOUGH LOVE
Prairie du Chien

Beneath the Crawford County Courthouse lies an unusual slice of territorial history: a jail that was built in 1843, though it could better be described as a dungeon.

The five largest cells measure only 5 by 7 feet. Each has a tiny window (wriggle out? no way!) and a bunk bed. Yes, *two* sorry souls shared this space no bigger than a bus shelter. Two cells are only 3 feet wide and have no bed—temporary holding cells, we have to hope. For the most miserable wretches, there was solitary confinement in two cells barely high enough to stand in, no window at all, and equipped with leg irons and arm chains. Something like a *Far Side* cartoon.

It's enough to make you watch your step around the courthouse. NO SMOKING. DON'T LITTER. Whatever you say, sir. Of course, the jail hasn't been in use since 1896, when a new one was built.

If you'd like to see the territorial jail, call the Crawford County clerk at (608) 326–0200 to arrange a tour. Recently the county replaced the original rubble floors with concrete to ensure safe footing for visitors.

CHIPS HAPPEN
Prairie du Sac

To the officials of the Wisconsin State Cow Chip Throw, the competitive tossing of dried cow manure would seem to be a serious matter: Contestants must select their chips from the wagonload provided by the Official Meadow Muffin Committee. Only two chips per contestant. Chips shall be at least 6 inches in diameter. No gloves. After all, a trip to the national championship in Beaver, Oklahoma, is at stake.

Ammunition for the Cow Chip Throw is collected from cow pastures by community-spirited volunteers, then sun-dried. Other annual events include the Tournament of Chips Parade, 5K and 10K runs, jugglers and magicians, arts and crafts, music and dancing, food and beer.

Kay Hankins of Prairie du Sac, an eight-time Cow Chip champion and a ten-time winner of the World Cow Chip Throw in Beaver, Oklahoma. Her overhead baseball throw and preference for heavier chips contributed to her long reign.

The event is held on Labor Day weekend. Follow the signs off business Highway 12 (Water Street) to Marion Park. Call (608) 643–4317 to inquire and register to throw. For more information see www.wiscowchip.com.

I N   W I S C O N S I N   W E   S A Y ,   " F O R W A R D ! "
R e t r e a t

A two-way parade—one that proceeds to the end of the parade route, turns around, and comes back—is extremely rare, but it's a regular feature of the World's Fair in the rural community of Retreat. Not only does the parade last longer that way, but you get to see both sides of the floats and the horses.

The parade starts at the old cheese factory and doubles back at Ames Feed Store, which is the extent of Retreat, or about half a mile. Retreat's population is small—too small to register on the census taker's radar—so neighbors like De Soto, a Mississippi River village just over the ridge, join in the grand procession. There are old and new farm machines, rescue vehicles, trucks of local businesses like a veterinarian and a septic system service, and original floats by school and church. A convertibleful of Vernon County royalty passes by, along with the De Soto High School marching band in maroon and gold. Gary Gilbertson provides live coverage for listeners tuned in to Viroqua's radio station WBRQ (1360 AM): "It's an amazing, amazing parade here at the Retreat World's Fair!"

At a pace of about 8 mph and with an intermission while the whole thing gets turned around (Retreat doesn't have any side streets—two-lane Highway N is *it*), the parade lasts about an hour. Afterward everyone lines up outside the food tent where lunch and hundreds of homemade pies await. Local talent presents a program on the wooden stage of the 1928 community building, and a horse show goes on all day. That night a dance ends the fair. People from all over come to the Retreat World's Fair, an annual event since 1919.

Retreat is on County Highway N in the southwest corner of beautiful Vernon County, and the fair is held on a Saturday in late September or early October. Find out when at www.visitvernoncounty.com.

MINER
TRANSGRESSIONS

*H*ighway U in Shullsburg is also known as Judge-ment Street. That and other street names (such as Truth, Peace, Charity, Faith, and Friendship) reflect the influence of Father Samuel Mazzuchelli, who, back in the 1800s, thought that it wouldn't hurt to remind the rowdy miners of this area of a few biblical virtues.

For insight into the miners' lives, you can visit an 1827 hand-dug lead mine and experience the small spaces and rugged working conditions. No wonder they acted out after a twelve-hour day down there. The Badger Mine and Museum are at the village park on West Estey Street, open daily from 10:00 A.M. to 4:00 P.M., Memorial Day through Labor Day. Call (608) 965–4860 for more information.

LAW OF GRAVITY REPEALED
Shullsburg

A short length of pavement on County Highway U south of Shullsburg is known far and wide as Gravity Hill. Farmers are used to seeing folks from all over creation out here on this little two-lane road, bean fields on both sides, lurching around as they stop their cars, back up, turn around, and try it again. The big attraction is the eerie sensation that occurs when your eyes say you're going downhill but your car says you're going uphill.

For the thrill of Gravity Hill, stop right here and shift into neutral.

To try it, start from the Shullsburg water tower. Your destination is only about 1 mile south. After you pass Rennick Road
on your left (at about %o mile) and are heading downhill, look
for a yellow, diamond-shaped sign with a black arrow and a 25
mph sign below. About three-fourths of the way to the bottom
of this hill but before you get to the sign, stop, put the car in
neutral, and feel it roll—uphill.

If you like optical illusions (if that's what it is), here are two
more. In Madison, from the top of O'Sheridan Street, keep your
eye on the capitol across Monona Bay and watch it get
smaller—appear to shrink away—instead of larger as you
approach it. (O'Sheridan is the first right off Lakeside Street
from John Nolen Drive.) At Maiden Rock, across Lake Pepin, is
Point–No Point, which appears to "melt away and fold back
into the bank," as Mark Twain described it. It helps to be on the
Mississippi River to appreciate this one.

Sun City
Soldiers Grove

Soldiers Grove, population 564, looks different from other
towns and villages in Crawford County. Buildings in the
business district on the south end of town have rooftop collec-
tors and skylights, and its streets have names like Solar Circle,
Passive Sun Drive, and Sunbeam Boulevard. It is the first, and
possibly the only, solar village in the United States.

After enduring several major floods, the people of Soldiers
Grove had had it up to here with the Kickapoo River, and they
had the high-water marks all up and down Main Street to
prove it. Rowing down Main Street wasn't funny anymore, and
pumping out the basement never had been. After another
major flood on Fourth of July weekend in 1978, they took the

high road: Instead of trying to control the river with dams and levees, they decided to move Soldiers Grove to higher ground. And while they were solving problems, such as the local economy, they adopted an ordinance that required new buildings to use the sun for at least half their heating needs. A study in 1991 concluded that the buildings are cost-effective.

Soldiers Grove is on County Highway 131 in the northeast corner of Crawford County.

L A S E R M O N K S
S p a r t a

The call for illuminated manuscripts has tapered off a lot over the past 900 years, so recently the monks of the Cistercian Abbey near Sparta updated the tradition. Operating under the name LaserMonks, they sell printing and imaging supplies for computers at big discounts.

The idea came to Father Bernard McCoy a few years ago when he was shopping for inkjet printer cartridges. Twenty-five or thirty dollars apiece struck him as a lot of money for that amount of black ink. It was the Barbie principle: Your first Barbie is not a big investment but it doesn't end there. It's everything you need to keep her going that runs into big money—Barbie's cheerleader outfits, her convertible, her beach house, her musical dream castle. Barbie is high-maintenance, and so are computers and copiers. Monks, on the other hand, are low-maintenance. Prayer, study, and Gregorian chants occupy much of the day at the Cistercian Abbey's picturesque rural setting (Barbie could take a lesson). The overhead is low, and that's the secret of LaserMonks's success.

Through arrangements with several large companies that make compatible and remanufactured products, LaserMonks, as an outsourcer, sells toner cartridges, inkjet cartridges, and copier toner at low prices, with satisfaction guaranteed and divine customer service. These monks aren't out to make a huge profit for themselves. They're real monks, unlike the ones who pitch breakfast bars and soft drinks in TV ads. The money goes to meet the expenses of the abbey and to support charities.

The idea of LaserMonks was to offer nonprofits an alternative to the high prices charged by the original equipment manufacturers (just as Barbie might get a better deal if she shopped somewhere besides Mattel). But business seems to have taken off, and Father Bernard might be in the mood to take on the big boys. You can cheer for David over Goliath at www.lasermonks.com.

WHERE GIANT SOMBREROS COME FROM
Sparta

Remember the huge hot pink frog with the slippery yellow tongue that you slid down about fifteen water parks ago? It came from the folks at FAST (Fiberglass Animals, Shapes, and Trademarks) in Sparta. So did the pelican slide and the Octoswing. Did you get a drink from the jaws of a hippo fountain, or gas up at the Sinclair station with the 40-foot dinosaur at the Dells? They came from here, too.

FAST specializes in gigantic theme-park creatures, landmarks, and trademarks, and it probably made your favorite, whether it's the 50-foot Jolly Green Giant in Blue Earth, Minnesota; the world's largest killer bee in Hidalgo, Texas; or the 200-foot sombrero in South Carolina—not to mention many of those chickens and clowns at fast food places. Even abroad you can't miss their work: the 26-foot pirate in

FAST, home of all creatures great and gargantuan.

Japan, the elk in Beirut, or the gorilla on a hillside in
Colombia, South America, where you can stand in its chest and
survey the water park below through a telescope. Furthermore,
since fiberglass lasts forever, your great-great-great-great-
grandchildren will be admiring all these things, too.

FAST is located just outside of Sparta on Highway 21 East
near Highway Q. It's worth cruising past headquarters to view
the graveyard of colossal roosters, cheeseburgers, hobos, and
Holsteins. Or see the awesome inventory at www.fastkorp.com.

THE HOUSE OF A GUY'S OWN
Spring Green

The House on the Rock is just a wee bit overdone. The carousel, for instance, has 20,000 lights, 182 chandeliers, 269 creatures (but not a single horse), and hundreds of mannequin-angels hovering and rotating overhead. There also are 250 dollhouses, miniature circuses with more than a million pieces, an organ console with fifteen keyboards, and tons of everything. At Christmas there are 6,000 Santas.

A tour of the extraordinary sixteen-building complex is like a movie made with a handheld camera. Is this room moving? The mix of music coming from all directions adds to the confusion, and together it has the quality of high school band practice.

By the time you stagger out three or four hours later, it's hard to name the strangest sight: The bushy eyebrows of a Fu Manchu drummer keeping time to "Danse Macabre" in the 2-story Mikado exhibit? The carrying case for a woman's artificial leg, inlaid with a Derringer pistol, in Unique Weaponry? The soaring pipes, catwalks, and massive machinery in the cavelike Organ Room, to the tune of the "Anniversary Waltz"? The curious tableaux taking place within the dollhouses? The plaintive sight of an empty little rowboat in the jaw of the 200-foot sea creature in the six-story Heritage of the Sea? Ronald Reagan in the trumpet section of the life-size, eighty-piece, automated circus orchestra?

The tour opens in the Japanese-style stone house that Alex Jordan began building in the 1940s. Then in his thirties, Jordan was a job-hopping, ex-student, ex–cab driver from Madison. He favored low ceilings, dim lighting, carpeted surfaces instead of furniture, and fireplaces. To add to the seductive effect, a phantom chamber orchestra of bows saws away at

*Circus musicians at House on the Rock wear
Dodgeville High School band uniforms.*

Ravel's "Bolero." Several more such rooms lead to daylight and
the Infinity Room, a 218-foot, glass-walled, cantilevered structure that soars out over the Wyoming Valley and offers a view
of the valley floor, fifteen stories straight down.

The "expansion phase" represents Jordan's eccentric obses-
sion to collect the largest, the biggest, and the most of whatever
he came across—dolls, clocks, violins, mirrors, paperweights,
weapons—and a place to put it all. Jordan never had enough of
anything, and what he couldn't collect, he created. "It doesn't
have to be good, it doesn't have to be bad, it just has to be,"
he often said. Much of what is here came from the on-site
workshop.

The House on the Rock is one of Wisconsin's most mind-boggling and popular attractions. Open daily from mid-March to the end of October, 9:00 A.M. to 6:00 P.M. (7:00 P.M. in summer). Also open in November and December for the scaled-down Christmas at House on the Rock. On Highway 23 between Spring Green and Dodgeville. Admission charge. Call (608) 935-3639 or visit www.houseontherock.com for details.

THE GARDEN OF EDEN

You can't have missed the fact, thanks to J. Heileman Brewing, that Wisconsin is God's Country, but did you know it also was the site of the Garden of Eden? According to the Reverend D. O. Van Slyke of Galesville, his own Trempealeau County along the Mississippi matched the biblical description perfectly—four rivers, surrounding bluffs, hanging gardens, milk, honey, apples, and plenty of snakes, albeit rattle.

Van Slyke was a circuit-riding preacher whose ministry included spreading the word about the discovery of Eden at the confluence of Highways 53 and 54 and drawing the faithful back to the state of innocence. His 1886 pamphlet Garden of Eden *made the case for the Wisconsin Eden, suggesting that Adam and Eve, having fallen from grace, moved to Minnesota (say, the Twin Cities—Sodom and Gomorrah?).*

When Eric Wallner started to build on his rural property north of Dodgeville, this is the first building he erected. With praying-hands roof, double doors with brass piano hinges, and parquet floor, it may be the only Prairie-style outhouse in the country. It also has a panoramic view of the countryside. Eric's new home (with indoor plumbing) is just a few miles from Taliesin, Frank Lloyd Wright's home and studio. He is an architect and has worked on Wright restorations.

So That's What Happened to Anne Baxter
Spring Green

Now why would a tree in honor of Hollywood actress Anne Baxter (1924–86) be growing in this rural cemetery, next to Unity Chapel? Because it's the Lloyd Jones family burial ground, and her mother, Catherine Wright Baxter, was architect Frank Lloyd Wright's first daughter, and Wright's mother was one of the "God-almighty Joneses," as the neighbors called them, for their highmindedness and tendency to preside over the countryside ("Truth against the world" was the family motto). Anne Baxter played such roles as Eve Harrington in *All About Eve* ("If nothing else, there's applause . . . like waves of love pouring over the footlights"), a princess of the Nile in *The Ten Commandments* ("Oh, Moses, you stubborn, splendid, adorable fool!"), and later on, for fun, Olga, Queen of the Cossacks, in several *Batman* episodes.

Frank Lloyd Wright's gravestone is here, but it marks an empty grave. He was buried here in 1959, but when his widow, Olgivanna, died in 1985, his body was removed and cremated so that his ashes could join hers at Taliesin West in Arizona, as her will specified.

The cemetery is 3 miles south of Spring Green, on County Highway T, east of Highway 23.

FIRST, SOAK ONE MOUNTAIN
Trempealeau

Trempealeau Mountain rises out of the Mississippi River just north of town. Appropriately enough, the name means "mountain soaking in water." It's a solid-rock island, the tallest of three island-mountains along the Mississippi.

The mountain was an important landmark for early steamboat pilots. Today river travelers are more likely to think of this point in the river as Lock and Dam Number 6, one of five on the Wisconsin side.

Lockmaster is not a job for your basic Type A personality. It takes about two hours for a towboat to maneuver a barge through the locks—if all goes well—and five days for the 669-mile trip between St. Paul and St. Louis. Picture yourself sharing the highway with the fifty-eight trucks it would take to transport the same amount of cargo and give the barge captain a big smile.

You can watch the action from an observation tower between the Mississippi and the railroad tracks that run parallel to the river. Apparently this is a principal north-south route; freight trains roar through here about every thirty or forty minutes. A biking and hiking trail is also nearby. All in all, this would be a good place for scouts to work on their Transportation badge.

A plywood replica of the 9,000-year-old mastodon that was found near the village of Boaz in 1897 often appears in parades in Richland County on a Lions Club trailer. One side is painted to look like hair, the other side like bones. The skeleton of the big bruiser now stands in the Geology Museum at the University of Wisconsin—Madison.

YOU'RE IN GOOD HANDS WITH HÜPEDEN
Valton

The community of Valton consists of just a handful of scattered buildings, and one of them is remarkable. On the outside, simple: white frame, 60 by 24 feet. On the inside, busy: every square inch is covered with a panoramic mural portraying the rituals and activities of the Modern Woodmen of America, a fraternal insurance society that flourished here around 1900.

It is the work of an itinerant landscape painter, Ernst Hüpeden, who arrived in Valton in 1897 and was hired to paint the stage curtain for the Woodmen Meeting Hall. The Woodmen were so pleased and impressed with the Mississippi River scene he produced that they asked him to continue. He agreed, in exchange for room and board and drink, according to one account of his life, which describes Hüpeden as "a colorful, tragic figure" whose past included emptying and painting whiskey bottles.

He went on to paint vivid scenes set in a pine forest that are both frightening depictions of injury and death (and life without life insurance?) and peaceful depictions of home life and fellowship among Woodmen. One scene shows a woman in mourning dress cashing in her insurance policy. Another reveals a curious initiation rite that involved strapping new members to a wooden goat on wheels and rolling them around the hall.

The Kohler Foundation funded the restoration of the Painted Forest. Valton is in northwestern Sauk County. Call (608) 983–2352 to arrange a visit, and see www.kohler foundation.org for directions.

CRANBERRY COMPETITION BOGS DOWN
Warrens

The annual Biggest Cranberry Contest is part of the three-day Warrens Cranberry Festival. Entries are judged by weight in grams. In case of a tie, the berries are measured for overall length, configuration, and originality of presentation to determine the winner.

Blue ribbons are awarded in ten different classes of cranberries. "Biggest Cranberry of Show" receives $25. ("Biggest" in 2002 weighed 5.08 grams. If that fails to impress you, weigh a few cranberries and read that line again.) Cranberries are displayed until the end of the festival on Sunday.

Wisconsin ranks first in U.S. cranberry production, and the Warrens gathering in late September is the largest cranberry festival in the world. It includes a parade, a fall produce market, several miles of antiques and crafts, bus tours of cranberry marshes, and even cranberry royalty—little tiny red round people with regal bearing. Festival information is available at www.cranfest.com or (608) 378–4200.

A LIVING FLAG
Witwen

The little community of Witwen consists of about twenty houses that face one another along two-lane Highway E. But neighbors come from miles around for Witwen's Fourth of July Parade. Lining up along the south edge of town, they

"She's a Grand Old Flag . . . " The Living Flag of Sauk County.

point their vans toward the cornfields, pop their hatches, and set up lawn chairs behind the white line.

The Sauk Prairie High School band plays "This Is My Country," the Busy Badgers and the Happy Hustlers 4-H Clubs toss candy from their floats, and a great deal of farm machinery rolls by. But the high point of the parade is the Living Flag, a row of seven women marching shoulder to shoulder, dressed in satin robes that line up to form Old Glory. The tradition was started about fifty years ago.

The women who march today are members of the Sauk County Home and Community Education Association. They occasionally appear at other Wisconsin events, parades, or centennial celebrations. (But not if it looks like rain. Raindrops ruin satin.) They've been featured in the national media ever since Charles Kuralt discovered them *On the Road* in 1980, and they appear in Kuralt's video *Seasons of America*.

Witwen is 7 miles west of Sauk City. The parade begins at 10:30 A.M., followed by a church-sponsored chicken barbeque and family entertainment.

INDEX

ABOUT THE AUTHORS

Michael Feldman has been doing radio for the better or worse part of twenty-plus years, most of it spent producing and hosting *Michael Feldman's Whad'Ya Know?* on Public Radio International. He lives in Madison, Wisconsin, with one wife, Sandy, two daughters, Ellie and Nora, and a yellow lab, Sugar.

Diana Cook researches the burning issues and inside dope for the cities of *Michael Feldman's Whad'Ya Know's* road shows and does freelance editorial work in Madison. Cook is the author of *Wisconsin Capitol: Fascinating Facts* and several features in *The Wisconsin Almanac,* and she recently revised and updated *Wisconsin Trivia.* She's also the mother of Andrew and Julia.

THE INSIDER'S SOURCE

FOR BOOKS TO YOUR AREA